Nathan

Albany

N. Y.

A

CONCISE TREATISE

ON

COMMERCIAL BOOK-KEEPING,

ELUCIDATING

THE PRINCIPLES AND PRACTICE OF DOUBLE ENTRY, AND THE
MODERN METHODS OF ARRANGING

MERCHANTS' ACCOUNTS.

By B. F. FOSTER.

Book-keeping is an art which no condition of life can render useless, which must contribute to the advancement of all who buy or sell — of all who wish to keep or improve their possessions — of all who desire to be rich, and all who desire to be wise. Let no man enter into business while he is ignorant of the method of regulating books. — *Dr. Johnson.*

SEVENTH EDITION.

BOSTON:
PUBLISHED BY T. R. MARVIN,
AND FOR SALE BY
PHILLIPS & SAMPSON, CHARLES TAPPAN,
AND B. B. MUSSEY.

1851.

PREFACE.

THE utility of Book-keeping is too obvious to be insisted upon. "There is no man," says Dr. Johnson, "who is not in some degree a merchant — who has not something to buy or something to sell, and who does not, therefore, want such instruction as may teach him to preserve his affairs from inextricable confusion."

Every individual must keep accounts in some manner; and in a country like ours, where men of enterprise often raise themselves from comparative indigence to affluence and wealth, a knowledge of Book-keeping is an object of the first importance to the rising generation as well as to the majority of adults. As a general study, this art is too much neglected. It is singular how little care is taken, even among merchants, to come at the right methods of practising it, and how few bestow any thing like that attention which it intrinsically merits. In Holland, it has become a proverb, that the man who fails in business did not understand accounts; and, in fact, nine cases of insolvency out of ten arise from want of method in keeping books.

The losses and embarrassments occasioned by its neglect, terminate so often in ruin, that it is equally the interest and duty of every person to make himself master of the most perfect and efficient system before entering upon the active pursuits of life. To the merchant, a knowledge of this art is absolutely indispensable; and the affairs of the mechanic, the lawyer, and the doctor, as well as the man of leisure, require a systematic, self-verifying record of accounts; — a want of which has ruined thousands of industrious and enterprising men.

Independently of its pecuniary advantages, the study of Book-keeping recommends itself as a means of intellectual culture, affording, as it

does, an ingenious and beautiful illustration of the harmony of method
and the use of numbers.

A practical knowledge of Book-keeping is considered by many
individuals as unattainable, except by attending for years to the daily
routine of the Counting-house. This opinion is certainly erroneous.
For, although every merchant has some peculiarities in the form or
arrangement of his books, yet the essentials are the same in all, and he
who has obtained a mastery of the fundamental and established principles of Double Entry, will scarcely find himself at a loss for twenty-
four hours in any Counting-house whatever.

The principal reason why so few succeed in obtaining a satisfactory
knowledge of Book-keeping at school, proceeds from the imperfect
manner in which it is taught, little or no pains being taken to illustrate
and explain the *principles* upon which the art is founded, in such a
manner that they may be clearly and fully comprehended.

The process of balancing the Ledger, and of adjusting the accounts,
the most difficult part of the science, is seldom understood.

The first and most important object to be attained by the student of
Book-keeping, is a clear and comprehensive knowledge of the nature
and arrangement of accounts in the Ledger. "The design of Book-
keeping," says Postlethwayt, "is to exhibit at all times a true state of
the merchant's affairs. The book in which this result is shown is
called the Ledger, which contains an abstract of every mercantile transaction arranged under distinct heads; so that if the reason of the entries
in the Ledger be once understood, the use of the Subsidiary Books and
the Journal will be so of course. *For it is the Ledger alone that can
teach the art, it being the most essential book.* The Subsidiary Books
may vary in number and form to suit the nature of the business; but,
in every instance, the principles and arrangement of the Ledger must
be the same. I am persuaded that the easiest, shortest, and most
effectual method to become skilled in this art is to obtain a complete
mastery of the Ledger first, and then proceed to its details." See
Chapter II., and Synopsis, pages 22 and 23.

The object of the present work is, to furnish schools and academies
with a treatise on Book-keeping, so simple in its illustrations as to be
easily understood by those who are unacquainted with the art; and
yet so comprehensive, as to afford all the information requisite for the

practical accountant. How far the author has been successful, is for others to decide. His aim has not been to promulgate new or fanciful theories; but rather to select information from the best sources, and to imbody the excellencies of the most approved writers upon the subject. The treatise of Morrison, which undoubtedly possesses great merit, is the basis of the present publication. The author is indebted to the able work of Cronhelm for many useful hints and much valuable matter. He has also made free use of the article Book-keeping, in McCulloch's Dictionary of Commerce, — written by one of the official assignees under the new British bankrupt act, — which, says McCulloch, " *exhibits a view of the art as actually practised in the most extensive houses in London."* The exemplifications in the following pages are conformable to the system there laid down ; and the rules and directions, it is believed, are not only full and explicit, but perspicuous and comprehensive. By divesting the science of numerous intricate terms and complicated entries, which never should be introduced in the puzzling form adopted by some authors, and by retaining such examples only as were necessary to elucidate its theory, the art is so simplified that its principles are easily comprehended, whilst their application to every transaction in trade is rendered apparent.

The author has given the most studious attention to the subject, and has availed himself of many favorable opportunities of becoming acquainted with the modern improvements in this art. And, in addition to several years' practice as book-keeper in an extensive mercantile establishment, he has had much experience in preparing young men for the business of the Counting-house. In the present work, he has endeavored to unite practical knowledge with elementary instruction, and to illustrate and exemplify the improvements which time and experience have effected in the arrangement and classification of merchants' accounts.

*A

CONTENTS.

SET I. — WHOLESALE DEALERS' BOOKS.

SET II. — MERCHANTS' ACCOUNTS EXEMPLIFIED.

BOOK-KEEPING.

CHAPTER I.

DEFINITIONS — SUBSIDIARY BOOKS — MERCHANTS' ACCOUNTS.

BOOK-KEEPING is the art of recording property in such a manner as to show its whole value collectively, and the value of each of its component parts.

That system of accounts which is called Double Entry, from the arrangement of its Ledger; and the Italian Method, from the country of its invention, in its primitive form, consisted of *three* books, viz.

I. The WASTE BOOK, which commences with an inventory of the merchant's Effects and Debts, and contains a simple narration of all his transactions, in the order of their occurrence.

II. The JOURNAL, which is merely a transcript of the Waste Book, with a formal statement of debtors and creditors resulting from each transaction.

III. The LEDGER, or register of the whole capital, as well as of each of its component parts.

In the earlier stages of commerce, the transactions of merchants were comparatively on a limited scale. The same individual did business in a variety of articles, but not to an extent

2

to require separate books for any particular branch of his mercantile operations.   Hence it was formerly the custom to record all purchases, sales, receipts, or payments, in a diary, which, from the rough manner of making the entries, was called 'The Waste Book,' or 'Blotter.'   But in all well-regulated establishments, at the present time, instead of *one*, several books are used for the original or primary entries, each appropriated to a distinct class of affairs.   For example, the receipts and payments of money are registered, as they occur, in the ' *Cash Book*,' or book for that special purpose ; and all bill transactions are first recorded in the ' *Bill Book*.'   This arrangement, therefore, always presents an unmixed and uninterrupted view of the cash and bill transactions.   The same principle of classification and subdivision is applicable to purchases, sales, shipments, consignments, and, in short, to every department of the most extensive and diversified business.

The Subsidiary Books, required by the *General Merchant*, are —

1. The *Cash Book*, containing cash transactions only.   On the left hand side, or folio, are entered all sums of money *received*, and on the right hand side, or folio, all sums *disbursed* or *paid out*.

2. The *Bill Book*, in one part of which are entered all bills receivable, and in the other all bills payable by the concern.[*]

3. The *Invoice Book*, which contains the particulars of goods purchased for exportation or otherwise.

4. The *Book of Shipments*, in which are entered the particulars of goods sent off, either in consequence of orders, or consigned for sale.

---

[*] All written obligations or engagements to pay money at a future period, such as bonds, promissory notes, drafts, or acceptances, are, in commercial language, called *Bills ;* those received and payable *to* the merchant are called ' *Bills Receivable ;*' and those issued by him, and for the payment of which he consequently becomes responsible, ' *Bills Payable.*'

5. The *Sales Book*, in which are entered the sales of goods on consignment, together with the charges incurred upon them, including the agent's commission.

The *Day Book* contains such occasional entries as do not, properly, belong to any one of the Subsidiary Books. It sometimes, however, contains the *amount* of purchases and shipments, with reference to the subordinate books for details.

The books here described are the authorities from which it is now customary to compose the JOURNAL. Their number indicates a division of counting-house work, to a considerable extent, and no where is such repartition productive of greater advantage. How much better is it to enter all bills in one book, and all cash transactions in another, than in any way to blend these very distinct entries! The effect of this subdivision is to simplify the Journal, in a manner highly conducive to accuracy and despatch, and to present such means of checking or examining each item, that transactions may be stated without liability to error.

The Subsidiary Books are varied in number, form, and arrangement, in every instance, according to the nature and extent of the business. It must not be supposed that all the books above enumerated are requisite in every establishment. In domestic or inland trade, where transactions are confined chiefly to purchases and sales, the principal books are the CASH BOOK, DAY BOOK, JOURNAL, and LEDGER.

There are, also, in every counting-house, a few books which do not form any part of the materials for the Journal, namely,

1. The *Account Current Book*, containing duplicates of accounts furnished to correspondents.
2. The *Letter Book*, containing copies of all important letters.
3. The *Petty Cash Book*, or account of petty disbursements.
4. The *Order Book*, containing copies of all orders received.
5. The *Cash Sales Book*, containing the cash sales of merchandise.

The accounts delivered by merchants to their customers or employers, are, *Bills of Parcels, Invoices, Account Sales,* and *Accounts Current.**

I. BILLS OF PARCELS.

A BILL OF PARCELS is a particular statement of goods when sold, containing the description, quantity, and price of each article; and the amount, with the place, date, and terms of credit. In making out such bills, the expression *Bought of* is always used; but for work done, money lent, or the like, the phrase *To* (A. B.) *Dr.* is substituted, as well as in general accounts. When the articles are sold and delivered at one time, the place and date are written at the top of the account; if not, the different dates are placed in the margin.

II. INVOICES.

An INVOICE is an account of goods sent off, generally by sea, either in consequence of an order from the person to whom they are sent, and at his risk, or consigned to him for sale at the risk of the shipper, with the marks of the packages exhibited on the margin, and the different charges attending the shipment *added* to the value of the goods, the sum of which is called the amount of the Invoice.

The preamble of an Invoice contains the names of the consigner and consignee; the names of the ship and master; the place from which she sails, and destination; and for whose account and risk the goods are shipped. Sometimes, for the satisfaction of the employers, the seller's Bills of Parcels are sent along with the goods, and only the amount of each bill is stated in the Invoice, with reference for particulars to the Bill of Parcels.

An Invoice ought to be made out with the utmost care, for it is a document of great importance in several respects; — first, between the exporting merchant and his correspondent; and next, when, in the hands of the latter, it generally forms a

---

* For a more extensive exemplification of merchants' accounts, promissory notes, bills, &c., the reader is referred to a work entitled ‘ *The Merchant's Manual,*’ published by Perkins & Marvin, Boston.

voucher for calculating import duty, if any, as well as for the sales effected to retailers or other dealers.

The sum insured usually exceeds the amount of the Invoice by two per cent., as the recovery of a loss from insurers involves a charge equal to that amount. It is thus necessary to cover not only the price of the goods and the charges at shipping, but such further sum as may enable the shipper, in case of loss, to recover the amount of the Invoice clear of any deductions.

III. Account Sales.

An Account Sales is a particular statement of goods sold on commission, transmitted by the agent to his employer, containing the name of the vessel by which the goods were received, and for whose account and risk they have been sold, with the charges attending the sale deducted from the total amount. Goods, when sent to an agent for sale, are said to be consigned to him. The person who sends the goods is called the *consigner*, the goods his *consignment,* and he to whom they are sent the *consignee.* The account transmitted by the consignee to the consigner is called an *Account Sales.* The sum that remains, after all charges have been deducted, is the *net proceeds,* which sum is due to the consigner.

The following abbreviations are used in merchants' accounts, namely — *Bo!* for bought; *Co.* for company; *Mdze.* for merchandise; *B. P.* for bill of parcels; *Rec.ᵈ Pay!* for received payment; *yds.* for yards; *p!* for pieces; *hhds.* for hogsheads; *bbls.* for barrels; *cwt.* for hundred weight; *qrs.* for quarters; *gro.* for gross; *ea.* for each; *@* for at, &c. *Shillings* are usually expressed by an oblique line, thus, */.* *C. B.* for Cash Book; *B. B.* for Bill Book; *S. B.* for Sales Book; *I. B.* for Invoice Book; *Dr.* for debtor; *Cr.* for creditor.

B

CHAPTER II.

THE LEDGER is the principal book of reference in the count-ing-house. It contains a synopsis of the merchant's affairs ; the several transactions being classified and arranged under distinct heads or accounts, in order that the state of any particular department, as well as the general result, may be readily ascer-tained.

One object of book-keeping is to show how the merchant's funds have been successively employed ; and, as property is in a state of continual change, it becomes necessary to have an exact register of these variations. Another object is to show the state of the concern commencing, the increase or decrease of the cap-ital from time to time, and the *sources* from which the gains and losses proceed. These objects are accomplished, first, by record-ing the whole capital collectively, and also the gains and losses ; and, secondly, by keeping a register of each investment or spec-ulation, so as to exhibit the outlay and returns. Hence an account must be opened, not only for every individual with whom the merchant has dealings *on credit*, but for every species of property which forms a constituent part of his capital, or which, by purchase or otherwise, comes into his possession.

The personal accounts are opened under their respective names ; the receipts and payments of money are classed under the title of ' Cash,' the bills and notes received under the title of ' Bills Receivable,' and those issued under the title of ' Bills Payable.'

14

When an Inventory of the Effects and Debts is taken, the whole mass or capital, abstracted from its constituent parts, is recorded under the title of ' Stock ;' and, in order that the capital may be presented in as simple a form as possible, the profits and losses are recorded in a separate account, which receives the double title of ' *Profit and Loss.*' In extensive concerns, accounts are also opened for ' Commission,' ' Charges,' ' Interest,' &c. ; and, as these are, in fact, simply branches of ' Profit and Loss,' their balances are transferred, periodically, to the latter account. All purchases and sales of goods may be classed under the general title of ' Merchandise ;' but, should the result of any particular investment be required, a separate account must be opened for it under some specific title.

Each account consists of two distinct parts. The space or folio being vertically divided, the *left* hand side is denominated DEBTOR, and the *right* CREDITOR. The positive parts, or Debit items, are entered in the left, and the negative parts, or Credit items, in the right hand money column.* The preposition *To* is prefixed to each entry on the left, and *By* to each entry on right hand side, thus : —

Dr.		CASH.			Cr.	
1839. Jan. 1. " 15.	To James Harrison, . . . To Henry Thompson, . .	500 150	00 00	1839. Jan. 8.	By Merchandise, ...	300	00

As the two sides of an account are of a contrary or opposite nature, to add to the one is equivalent to subtracting from the other.

---

* Positive and negative are relative terms, implying, in this case, that one item is placed in opposition to another. When several quantities enter into a calculation, it is frequently necessary that some parts should be added, and others subtracted. The former are called *positive,* and the latter *negative.* For instance, in estimating the profits of a concern, if the gain be positive, the loss will be negative ; because the loss must be deducted from the gain, to determine the net profit. A merchant's effects may be considered as positive, and his debts as negative, parts of his capital ; for the debts must be subtracted from the effects, in order to ascertain his real worth.

The abbreviations DR. and CR. *are used merely to distinguish the left from the right hand side of an account.*

When applied to *persons*, *Dr.* signifies that the individual is indebted for all sums in the left, and *Cr.* that the concern is indebted to him for all sums in the right hand money column; but, with this exception,* these terms must not be understood to mean, in an absolute manner, that we *owe*, or that any thing *owes* us.   The accounts of Cash, Bills Receivable, Bills Payable, Merchandise, Stock, Profit and Loss, and the like, simply exhibit the permutations or changes which the capital undergoes in the course of business.   Thus the *Dr.* side of 'Cash' shows receipts, and the *Cr.* side disbursements, of money ; the *Dr.* side of 'Bills Receivable' shows the bills received, and the *Cr.* side the amount of such bills as have been disposed of; the *Cr.* side of 'Bills Payable' shows the bills issued, and the *Dr.* side all such bills as have been retired from circulation.

The *Dr.* side of 'Merchandise' shows its cost or value, and the *Cr.* side the sales or returns.   'Stock' account is designed to exhibit the assets and liabilities of the concern, abstractly considered ; and 'Profit and Loss,' with its ramifications, is simply a branch of 'Stock,' its object being to collect the several augmentations and diminutions of the capital.

It is indispensably necessary, therefore, that the nature and purpose of each class of accounts should be distinctly understood, and clearly comprehended, by the learner, at the ouset, without which his knowledge must be superficial, imperfect, and of no practical utility.

The mutual relations of Debtor and Creditor are developed in the LEDGER *only*, — the Subsidiary Books and the Journal being merely preparatory steps, totally unconnected with the *principles* and *proof* of accounts ; and although, in the order of writing, the Journal precedes the Ledger, yet, from the nature of the case, it is impossible for the learner to comprehend the process of journalizing, unless the arrangement and classification of the Ledger are *previously* understood.   Hence it is this to which

---

* '*Bills Receivable*,' and '*Bills Payable*,' are substituted *personal* accounts, showing the amount due to or by the concern, *in the shape of bills*. See Note, page 10.

his attention should be first, and chiefly, and most assiduously, directed.

The accountant always considers the effect of an entry as it regards the Ledger, which naturally leads him to select the true Debtors and Creditors; therefore, whoever would be fundamentally grounded in this science should not perplex himself with any other book *till he is perfectly master of the Ledger.*

In order to obtain a thorough and satisfactory knowledge of book-keeping, it is important, before we proceed to its details, to investigate the real *principles* of the art, and to disentangle them from *forms*, with which they are too often confounded.

It is a primary axiom of the exact sciences, that "the whole is equal to the sum of its parts," and this axiom constitutes the basis of *Double Entry.* In the classification of this system, property is regarded as a whole, composed of various parts. The component parts are Cash, Bills Receivable, Debts Receivable, Goods, &c. The whole mass is technically called Stock.

The Stock Account records the *whole* capital, without designating its parts; the Money, Personal, and Property Accounts record its constituent parts. Hence the *parts* and the *whole* mutually check and verify each other; for, whatever variations they undergo, and whether the capital increase, decrease, or remain stationary, it must constantly equal the collective result of those parts.

It is this peculiar arrangement which constitutes what is called DOUBLE ENTRY, and which enables the merchant to ascertain his real worth, or net capital, by *two* distinct processes; first, by reference to the Stock Account; and, secondly, by a collection of its component parts, — *the exact agreement of the two results proving the accuracy of the books.*

For an illustration of this principle, let us suppose a merchant's capital to consist of the following items, viz.

Cash,	in hand,	10,000
Merchandise,	valued at	7,000
Henry Brown	owes	3,000
Net Capital,		$ 20,000

In this case, we enter the whole amount, in one mass, to the

3   B *

credit of 'Stock,' and debit 'Cash,' 'Merchandise,' and 'Henry Brown,' for its constituent parts, thus : —

Dr.	S T O C K.				*Cr.*	
					20,000	00

Dr.	C A S H.				*Cr.*	
	10,000	00				

Dr.	M E R C H A N D I S E.				*Cr.*	
	7,000	00				

Dr.	H E N R Y B R O W N.				*Cr.*	
	3,000	00				

From this view of property, as a whole constantly equal to the sum of its parts, we now ascend to a higher and more general consideration of it, as a mass of relations between Debtors and Creditors. The application of these terms was originally personal; but it is extended by analogy to every part of property, and to the whole capital itself.

Debtor and Creditor are correlative; — the one implies and involves the other, and cannot exist without it. Hence every transaction in business belongs to at least *two* accounts, and must be entered to the debit of one, and to the credit of the other. When, for example, a person becomes indebted to me, the sum is entered to his *debit*. If for money, it is also entered to the *credit* of 'Cash;' if for goods, to the *credit* of 'Merchandise:' or, in whatever way the debt arises, it is entered on the *credit* side of some other account.   On the contrary, when I become indebted to an individual, the amount is placed to his *credit*: if for money, it is also entered to the *debit* of 'Cash;' if for goods, to the debit of 'Merchandise.'   Consequently, every item in an account has its counterpart; that is, it corresponds to some other item on the opposite side of a different account; and it follows, *that if all the accounts be added, the aggregate of the Debtor sides of the Ledger will equal that of the Creditor sides.*

In tracing the principle of equality, we have considered property in a state of rest; but we shall find it equally essential to property in motion.   This is evident from two considerations.

1. At any two periods — as the beginning and the end of a year — the equilibrium of debtors and creditors exists in the concern, considered in a state of rest.   From the axioms, that if equals be added to equals, the sums will be equal; or, if equals be taken from equals, the remainders will be equal; it is evident that the same equilibrium must exist in all the intermediate occurrences.

2. The same thing is apparent from the very nature of mercantile transactions.   The component parts of property are in a state of continual change.   In purchases, cash is converted into goods; and in sales, goods are reconverted into cash.   Or, if credit is allowed, the changes are still more numerous.   Purchases create creditors; sales convert goods into debtors; receipts convert personal debtors into cash, whilst payments destroy cash and personal creditors.   The introduction of bills would multiply the changes by an intermediate stage between personal debts and cash.   But all these metamorphoses and destruction of the parts, resolve themselves into the single case, *that, in every transaction, two accounts are affected, the one receiving what the other communicates.*   The *imparting* account is always CREDITOR, and the *recipient* account always DEBTOR; so that debtor and creditor must perfectly equilibrate.

We proceed to show that this equality of debtors and creditors is not disturbed by profits and losses, or, in other words, by the augmentations and diminutions of the capital.   Each alteration in the *whole* can be produced only by a correspondent alteration in one of its *parts ;* and hence two accounts are always affected by the change. Thus, when the sale of goods exceeds the cost, 'Merchandise' is debtor for the gain, and 'Stock' is creditor ; when the sale falls short of the cost, 'Merchandise' is creditor for the loss, and 'Stock' is debtor. In these cases, there is a transfer between the whole and its parts, the one receiving what the other transmits ; but, as it would be inconvenient to record in the *Stock* account every individual alteration of capital, the *transfer is made periodically ;* and when the profits and losses proceed from various sources, accounts are opened to collect the particulars and transmit the general result in one entry to ' Stock.'

Till the time of this transfer, the profits and losses remain latent in the particular accounts, without at all disturbing the equality of debtors and creditors. Thus, goods bought of A for $900, and sold to B for $1,000, leave a profit of $100, which remains latent in the ' Merchandise ' account till the periodical transfer. Debtors and creditors are, in the mean time, perfectly equilibrated ; for, in the purchase, ' Merchandise ' is debtor $900, and A is creditor $900 ; whilst, in the sale, ' Merchandise ' is creditor $1,000, and B is debtor $1,000.

The equilibrium of debtors and creditors having been demonstrated, as well from the nature of these relations as from the axiom that the whole is equal to the sum of its parts ; and having been shown to exist essentially in property, in every state, whether of motion or of rest, we may justly lay it down *as the fundamental principle of book-keeping — a principle not of art or invention, but of science and discovery ; not of mere expediency, but of absolute necessity, and inseparable from the nature of accounts.*

———

Without entering into subdivisions, it will be sufficient to enumerate the objects of book-keeping under four *general* heads, viz.

1. STOCK ACCOUNT.
2. MONEY ACCOUNTS.
3. MERCHANDISE ACCOUNTS.
4. PERSONAL ACCOUNTS.

The record of each class of accounts is essential to the cor rectness of the science ; for, whenever one of the parts of property is omitted, the system must, of necessity, be partial and incomplete ; there can be no dependence or harmony between the whole and the parts ; the stock or capital cannot be ascertained from the accounts alone, and, when it is obtained by valuations and inventories, it will stand unconnected and unproved in the books.

The details of book-keeping may be varied according to the nature of the business ; but there are, properly speaking, only two methods which differ materially from each other, namely, SINGLE and DOUBLE ENTRY.

In Single Entry, an enumeration of the effects and debts is made, in order to discover the Capital. In Double Entry, the Capital is ascertained by two processes ; — first, by the STOCK ACCOUNT ; secondly, by collecting its component parts. Single Entry is imperfect in some particulars, as it records personal accounts only ; hence, the *gain* or *loss* cannot be known till the debts and effects are collected, and it is then obtained by a comparison with the original capital. In Double Entry, the *gain* or *loss* is declared by the Profit and Loss Account, independently of the general extract or balance.

Double Entry has more advantages to a merchant than to a retail dealer, because his transactions are more extensive and complicated ; and it shows in what manner his funds have been successively invested. As every debtor has a creditor, no part of his property is unaccounted for ; and, when in doubt as to any specific portion, he will find a solution of the difficulty in his own Ledger. Those who know how soon money becomes absorbed, and in how few years large sums may be invested in machinery, shipping, or other fixed capital, are aware that merchants would often be deceived, if they had not, at all times, an unfailing clew to the appropriation of their capital.

SYNOPSIS

OF THE

CLASSIFICATION AND ARRANGEMENT

OF

ACCOUNTS IN THE LEDGER.

Dr.   S T O C K .   *Cr.*

The object of this account is to exhibit the Assets and Liabilities in one mass. It records the *whole* Capital, without designating its constituent parts.

The total sum of the debts, or liabilities, if any, is entered in the left-hand column, or Dr. side.	The total sum of the assets, or effects, is entered in the right-hand column, or Cr. side.

₊ If the *Cr.* side be greatest, the balance, or difference, is the *net capital*; but if the *Dr.* side exceed the *Cr.*, the concern is, of course, *insolvent*, and the difference shows the *deficiency*.

Dr.   P R O F I T   A N D   L O S S .   *Cr.*

The object of this account is to collect the Gains and Losses on the business.

The several items of loss are entered in the left-hand column, or Dr. side; and	The several items of gain are entered in the right-hand column, or Cr. side.

₊ The difference is the net gain or loss, as the case may be, which, at every general balance, is transferred to the *Stock* account.

Dr.   M E R C H A N D I S E .   *Cr.*

The object of this account is to show the gain or loss on Merchandise.

The cost, or value of all goods purchased, is entered on the Dr. side; and	The sales of all goods, or other returns, are entered on the Cr. side.

₊ The value of the goods *unsold* is the BALANCE, and must be placed on the Cr. side; the difference is gain or loss.

Dr. <div align="center">C A S H .</div> *Cr.*

The object of this account is simply to show the *Cash* in hand.

The cash in hand, when the books are opened, and all sums received, are entered on the Dr. side ; and	The several disbursements, or sums of money paid out, are entered on the Cr. side.

₄ The difference between the two sides is the BALANCE of Cash.

Dr. <div align="center">B I L L S   R E C E I V A B L E .</div> *Cr.*

The object of this account is to show the *Bills, Notes, Bonds,* &c., unpaid.

The amount on hand at the beginning, and all bills which the merchant receives, are entered in the Dr. column ; and	The amount of every such bill disposed of, or for which he receives payment, is entered in the Cr. column.

₄ The difference is the amount due *to* the concern in the shape of notes, bills, &c.

Dr. <div align="center">B I L L S   P A Y A B L E .</div> *Cr.*

The object of this account is to show the merchant's *Liabilities,* in the shape of *promissory notes* or *acceptances.*

The amount of all such bills as are paid, or retired from circulation, is entered on the Dr. side.	The amount of all notes or acceptances issued by the concern is entered on the Cr. side ; and

₄ The difference is what the concern *owes* in notes or acceptances.

Dr. <div align="center">A . B .</div> *Cr.*

The object of an individual's account is to show what is due, either *to* or *by* him, as the case may be.

All sums for which he is indebted are entered on the left-hand or Dr. side of his account ; and	All sums for which the *concern* is indebted to him are entered on the right-hand or Cr. side.

₄ The difference is what he owes, or what the concern owes him.

' Stock,' ' Profit and Loss,' ' Merchandise,' ' Cash,' ' Bills Receivable,' ' Bills Payable,' and the Personal Accounts, are common to almost every description of commercial business ; but when goods are consigned to another for sale and returns, or when a merchant transacts business as an agent or factor, it becomes necessary to create a distinct class of accounts, which are not required in inland or domestic trade.

For example, if I intrust goods to a commission house, to sell on my account and risk, or, which amounts to the same thing, ship goods abroad on consignment, it is obvious that the agent, or person to whom they are shipped, ought not to be *debited* for the cost of such shipment ; he is only responsible for the goods he sells, after deducting his commission, &c. In this case, however, the property has gone out of my possession, and must be recorded in such a manner as to show its cost, and the circumstances under which it is situated. For this purpose, it is usual to open an account for each consignment under some appropriate title — such as, ' Shipment to ——,' or ' Adventure to ——,' (naming the place,) or ' Consignment per ——,' (naming the ship,) — which is debited for the cost or value of the goods and all charges incurred upon the shipment, and credited, when the account sales is received, for the returns or net proceeds.

On the contrary, if goods are consigned to me for sale, on behalf of an employer, it is evident, *as they do not belong to me,* that their cost should not be entered on the *Dr.* side of my Ledger ; but when I sell any quantity of these goods, I am then accountable for the amount sold, after deducting commission and charges. In such transactions, an account is usually opened for each individual's consignment under some definite title — as, ' A. B.'s Sales,' or ' Sales No. 1,' ' Sales No. 2,' &c. ; or ' Sales per Ship ——,' (naming her) — which accounts are debited for the several charges incurred, including commission, and credited for the sales as they occur.

Instead of opening separate accounts in the Ledger for each consignment, some book-keepers open only *one* account for all goods sold on commission, under the general title of ' Sales of Consignments,' and refer to the Sales Book for the particulars.

The following will serve to exemplify the arrangement of this class of accounts : —

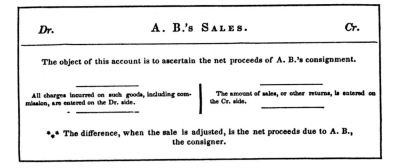

Dr.	ADVENTURE TO ———.	Cr.
	The object of this account is to show the gain or loss on the shipment or adventure.	
The whole cost of the goods, including charges, is entered on the Dr. side ; and		The returns, or net proceeds, are entered on the Cr. side.
	₊ The difference, when all the goods are sold, is the gain or loss.	

In joint adventures or company accounts, when you are the manager, and furnish the goods, debit your partners personally for their respective shares, and the shipment, under its proper title, for your share ; but when you are not the manager, enter your share only.

Dr.	A. B.'s SALES.	Cr.
	The object of this account is to ascertain the net proceeds of A. B.'s consignment.	
All charges incurred on such goods, including commission, are entered on the Dr. side.		The amount of sales, or other returns, is entered on the Cr. side.
	₊ The difference, when the sale is adjusted, is the net proceeds due to A. B., the consigner.	

Every description of *outlay*, for which no return is to be received, or of *income*, for which no property is exchanged, — such as store-rent, postages, interest, commission, &c., — must have an account opened for it in the Ledger ; but if the *general* result only is required, this class of receipts and expenditures may be entered at once in the general account of 'Profit and Loss.'

4   c

The accounts of 'Commission,' 'Interest,' 'Charges,' and the like, are merely subdivisions of 'Profit and Loss,' and the latter is simply a branch of 'Stock.'

On the *Cr.* side of ' *Commission* ' are entered all sums received for transacting business for others. There are seldom any entries on the *Dr.* side ; the result is, therefore, gain, and is transferred to ' Profit and Loss.'

On the *Dr.* side of ' *Interest* ' are entered all sums paid, and on the *Cr.* side all sums received, by the merchant for interest or discounts.

On the *Dr.* side of ' *Charges* ' are entered all sums paid for rents, clerks' salaries, postages, advertising, &c., and on the *Cr.* side all sums which are charged to correspondents for postages, &c. The result of the two last accounts is transferred, at every general balance, to ' Profit and Loss.'

Every amount, or sum, entered in the Ledger, must be placed on the *Dr.* side of one or more accounts, and on the *Cr.* side of some other account or accounts. *This rule is absolute and universal.*

One of the fundamental and indispensable laws of Double Entry is, that every discharge must be *specific.* When the account is with *persons*, the discharge answers in *value* to the charge ; but when the account is of *things*, the discharge must answer in *kind.*

Thus, in opening an account for any species of property, the name or title is, in the first instance, perfectly arbitrary ; but when a title is once selected, all subsequent entries which relate to it must be made in accordance with the original entry. For instance, suppose I purchase 500 barrels of flour, I may place the cost or value to the debit of the general account of ' Merchandise,' or open a particular account for this article alone, under the title of ' *Flour ;* ' but when I dispose of this flour, I am not at liberty to credit, at pleasure, either of these accounts for the returns — *I must credit the one originally charged.*

CHAPTER III.

THE JOURNAL contains a concise statement of the several transactions which are recorded in the daily or subordinate books, with the *Drs.* and *Crs.* so arranged that each amount may be easily transferred to the Ledger. The process of transcribing the entries into this book is technically called *Journalizing.* The indispensable condition of every Journal entry is, that the debit and credit amounts must be exactly equal.

When a transaction is to be Journalized, first consider to what account in the *Ledger* it must be placed, both on the *Dr.* and *Cr.* sides, which will immediately suggest the correct form and arrangement of the entry ; and, although the term *Cr.* is never expressed in the *Journal,* yet it is always understood to follow the preposition *to.* Thus the entry,

CASH *Dr. to* MERCHANDISE,............................$ 500

signifies that 'Cash' is to be *debited* $ 500, and 'Merchandise' *credited* for the same sum.

All the difficulties of Journalizing will be overcome, as soon as the learner obtains clear and definite notions of the scheme and arrangement of the Ledger.

EXAMPLES.

1. — Bought a quantity of *goods,* for *cash,* amounting,
     ℣ invoice, to..................................$ 1,000

All *purchases* of goods are entered on the *Dr.* side of 'Merchandise,' and all *disbursements* of money on the *Cr.* side of ' Cash ; ' therefore, in Journalizing this entry, we say,

> MERCHANDISE *Dr. to* CASH,
> Purchased this day, ℈ invoice,...........................$ 1,000

The simple meaning of this entry is, that, in the Ledger, ' Merchandise ' is to be debited * ' *To Cash*, $ 1,000,' and ' Cash ' credited ' *By Merchandise*, $ 1,000.'

> 2. — Sold, for *cash*, a quantity of goods, amounting to.......$ 1,500

All moneys *received* are entered on the *Dr.* side of ' Cash,' and all *sales* of goods on the *Cr.* side of ' Merchandise ; ' hence, in Journalizing the second entry, we say,

> CASH *Dr. to* MERCHANDISE,
> For sales this day,...................................$ 1,500

the meaning of which is, that ' Cash ' is to be debited ' *To Merchandise*, $ 1,500,' and ' Merchandise ' is to be credited ' *By Cash*, $ 1,500.'

> 3. — Bought of Charles Harrison, *on credit*, sundry *goods*,
> amounting to...................................$ 800

In this transaction, I am indebted to Harrison $ 800, for which value has been received in goods.   The Journal entry is,

> MERCHANDISE *Dr. to* CHARLES HARRISON,
> For goods purchased of him,............................$ 800

The *Cr.* side of each individual's account shows what the concern owes him ; and hence this entry signifies that ' Merchandise ' is to be debited ' *To Charles Harrison*, $ 800,' and that Harrison is to be credited ' *By Merchandise*, $ 800.'

---

* To *debit* an account means, to enter a sum on the *Dr.* or left-hand side of the Ledger ; and to *credit* an account means, to enter the sum on the *Cr.* or right hand side.

4. — Sold James Bruce & Co., at 90 days' credit, 15 pieces
   Broadcloth,......:............................$ 1,350

When a person gets into my debt, the amount must be placed on the *Dr.* side of his account; therefore, in Journalizing this sale, we say,

JAMES BRUCE & Co. *Dr. to* MERCHANDISE,
For 15 pieces Broadcloth, amounting to.................$ 1,350

which signifies that James Bruce & Co. are to be debited ' *To Merchandise,* $ 1,350,' and ' Merchandise ' credited ' *By J. Bruce & Co.,* $ 1,350.'

5. — Accepted Charles Harrison's draft on me, payable at
   30 days' date, due Feb. 4th, ...$ 800

All notes, drafts, or acceptances, which the merchant *issues*, are entered on the *Cr* side of ' Bills Payable.' The Journal entry is,

CHARLES HARRISON *Dr. to* BILLS PAYABLE,
For my acceptance, at 30 days,........................$ 800

The meaning of this entry is, that Charles Harrison is to be debited ' *To Bills Payable*, $ 800,' and ' Bills Payable ' credited ' *By Charles Harrison*, $ 800.' This transaction is merely a transfer of a debt from Harrison, with whom it was originally contracted, to the holder of my acceptance. I therefore debit the former in the account bearing his name, and credit the latter in a general account, which I open for all such obligations. ' Bills Payable ' is managed precisely like a personal account ; namely, it is credited for all the merchant's *liabilities*, in the shape of notes, acceptances, &c., and debited for such of these as are paid or withdrawn from circulation. It need scarcely be observed, that nothing can be entered to the debit of ' *Bills Payable*,' except what has first been placed to its credit ; for, before a bill can be redeemed, it must have been issued.

6. — Received of James Bruce & Co. their promissory
   note, at 90 days' date, due March 3d,...............$ 1,350

c *

All notes, drafts, or acceptances, which the merchant *receives,*
are entered on the *Dr.* side of ' Bills Receivable.'   Bruce & Co.
have cancelled their book debt, and are responsible only to the
holder of their note for this amount.   Hence, in Journalizing
the preceding entry, we say,

> BILLS RECEIVABLE *Dr. to* J. BRUCE & Co.
> For their bill, at 90 days' date, due 3d March,.............$ 1,350

This is merely a transfer between two accounts, and means that
' Bills Receivable' is to be debited ' *To J. Bruce & Co.,* $ 1,350,'
and that J. Bruce & Co. are to be credited ' *By Bills Receivable,*
$ 1,350.'

> 7. — *Paid* my acceptance in favor of C. Harrison, due Feb. 4th, $ 800

When a debt or obligation is entered on the *Cr.* side of any
particular account, it must be entered on the *Dr.* side of the
same account, when it is paid or otherwise discharged ; and *vice
versa.*   This bill, when *issued,* was entered on the *Cr.* side of
' Bills Payable ; ' and therefore, in the Journal, we say,

> BILLS PAYABLE *Dr. to* CASH,
> Paid my acceptance favor Harrison,.....................$ 800

It is obvious that this, like the above, is simply a transfer between
two accounts : the meaning is that ' Bills Payable' is to be debited ' *To Cash,* $ 800,' and ' Cash ' credited ' *By Bills Payable,*
$ 800.'

> 8. — James Bruce & Co. have paid their promissory note, due
> March 3d, in cash,................................$ 1,350

This transaction is also a simple transfer between two accounts,
namely, the receipt of cash and the disposal of a bill.   The
Journal entry is,

> CASH *Dr. to* BILLS RECEIVABLE,
> Received for Bruce & Co.'s bill,......................$ 1,350

The foregoing examples are *simple* Journal entries. A *compound* entry is one in which there are two or more debtors to the same creditor, or two or more creditors to the same debtor, as is often the case when five or six sales are made to as many different persons, or a like number of purchases, payments, &c., occurring at the same date, or even at different dates. For instance : —

9. — Sold *goods* this day to the following persons, at 90 days' credit, ⅌ Sales Book, viz.

James Thompson,...............................	$ 150
Henry Brown,...................................	365
Thomas Smith,.................................	485
	$ 1,000

In this transaction, 'Merchandise' is to be credited for the amount sold, $1,000, and each personal account debited for its respective share. In the Journal, we say,

SUNDRIES *Dr. to* MERCHANDISE,
    For sales this day, ⅌ S. B.

James Thompson,.......................................	$ 150
Henry Brown,..	365
Thomas Smith, ...	485
	$ 1,000

The term *Sundries,* in all such cases as the above, means two or more *accounts.* Thus, instead of saying, 'J. Thompson Dr. to Merchandise,' 'Henry Brown Dr. to Merchandise,' and 'Thomas Smith Dr. to Merchandise,' we avoid this repetition by using the word *Sundries ;* and then each individual is debited for his particular proportion, and 'Merchandise' credited for the *whole* amount.

10. — Bought goods of the following persons, this day, on credit, as ⅌ invoices, viz.

C. Hammond,...................................	100
Buchanan & Co...............................	1,200
James Finlay & Co...........................	1,300
	$ 2,600

In Journalizing this transaction, we say,

> MERCHANDISE *Dr. to* SUNDRIES,
> For purchases this day.
> To C. Hammond, ... 100
> To Buchanan & Co.................................... 1,200
> To James Finlay & Co................................ 1,300
> $ 2,600

The term Sundries is here used merely to avoid recapitulating the same creditor, and, of course, no such account is opened in the Ledger as ' *Sundries.*' The obvious and only meaning of the foregoing entry is, that the account of ' Merchandise ' must be debited ' *To Sundries,* $2,600,' and each of the Personal Accounts credited ' *By Merchandise,*' for its proportion, so that the aggregate of the credit items will equal the debit amount.

In complex entries, it is often expedient to class two or more debit items against several credit items, — even when the respective amounts are various, — by prefacing the entry thus, ' *Sundries* Dr. to *Sundries,*' and then describing three or four debtors against eight or ten creditors. The following will serve as an exemplification : —

> 11. — SHIPPED ℔ the Spooner, for Jamaica, by order, and on account and risk, of the following persons, ℔ Invoice Book.
>
> *For John Stirling,*
>> Goods,...........amounting to...........2,050
>> Charges,.........paid at shipping,........ 225
>> Commission, ...on goods, &c.,.......... 52
>> Insurance,........on $ 2,400,............. 50 — 2,377 00
>
> *For Murray & Co.,*
>> Goods,...........amounting to...........4,000
>> Charges,.........paid at shipping,........ 314
>> Commission,......on goods, &c.,.......... 100
>> Insurance,........on $ 4,600,............. 86 — 4,500 00
>> $ 6,877 00

The above shipment might, with propriety, be Journalized similar to example 10, by making J. Stirling Dr. to Sundries for the amount of his invoice, and Murray & Co. Dr. to Sundries for the amount of their invoice ; but several postings to the Ledger are avoided, and the Journal entry made equally simple, by the following arrangement : —

SUNDRIES *Dr. to* SUNDRIES.*

For shipment ℔ Spooner.

— *Drs.* —

John Stirling,..........for amount of invoice,..........	2,377 00
Murray & Co.......... " " " "	4,500 00
	$ 6,877 00

— *Crs.* —

To Merchandise,........................	6,050 00
To Charges,............................	539 00
To Commission,.........................	152 00
To Insurance,..........................	136 00
	$ 6,877 00

By the above arrangement, it will be seen that the goods, charges, &c., form but one sum in the *Cr.* items ; that is, the goods shipped to Stirling, and to Murray & Co., amount, when added, to the sum of $ 6,050 ; the charges paid for *both firms*, to $ 539 ; the commission to $ 152 ; and the insurance to $ 136.

The title or preface to the *Journal* entries always has reference to the Ledger. For instance, in posting the last example, we turn to Stirling's account, and enter on the debit side, ' *To Sundries*, $ 2,377 ; ' and also to Murray & Co.'s account, and enter, as before, ' *To Sundries*, $ 4,500.' We next turn to the accounts which are to be credited, and write ' *By Sundries*, . . . ,' each for its respective amount.

———

To find the *Drs.* and *Crs.*, observe, in every transaction, whether a person has become indebted to you, or you to him ; whether property has been received or delivered ; and whether you have gained or lost upon any account. The following rules

---

* This is an abbreviated title. Its full meaning is, ' Sundry Accounts Dr. to Sundry Accounts.'

5

being applied to the result of these observations, the debtors and creditors may easily be ascertained : —

GENERAL RULES.

The thing received is Dr. to the thing delivered ; or,

The thing *received*, or person accountable to you, is.................*Dr.*
The thing *delivered*, or person to whom you are accountable, is....... *Cr.*

1. *The Accounts of Persons*
are *debited* when persons become indebted to you, and *credited* when you become indebted to them.

2. *The Accounts of Money*
are *debited* for all sums *received*, and *credited* for all disbursements or sums *paid*.

3. *The Accounts of Property*
are *debited* when, by purchase, property comes into your possession, and *credited* when it goes out of your possession.

4. *Profit and Loss,*
(Or its Subsidiary Accounts,)
is *debited* for every *loss* or charge against the business, and *credited* for every *gain*.

The *rules* for distinguishing the *Drs.* and *Crs.* in any particular entry, are inferred from *the nature of the accounts in the Ledger ;* but rules should never usurp the place of *reasons.* The student of book-keeping must be made to think for himself. That plan of instruction which dwells long on *first principles* will be the most effectual. Experience has shown, that, whenever a question arises which is not anticipated in the book, none but the student whose mind has been exercised in the investigation of truth, — who is the *master*, and not the *slave*, of rules, — will solve an unexpected difficulty by a novel application of the principles of the science.

CHAPTER IV.

THE JOURNAL, being an abstract of the Subsidiary Books, is
completed monthly. While, in the Cash Book, every receipt or
payment is entered the day it takes place, and, in the Bill Book,
every bill is entered the day it is received or issued, the Journal
entries are classified and condensed so as to comprise in one
amount a number of similar transactions occurring at different
dates. Thus, the collective entry of ' *Cash Dr. to Sundries* '
exhibits, successively, all the receipts of money during the month,
the total of which is carried to the debit of ' Cash ; ' and the
collective entry of ' *Sundries Dr. to Cash* ' exhibits, in like
manner, all the payments of money, the *aggregate* alone being
posted to the credit of ' Cash.' The same combination of
entries is made in reference to every department of business : all
similar items relating to each account are classed together, and
posted in one sum to the Ledger. By this arrangement, the
Ledger is so abridged that, in most cases, not more than twelve
lines are required for each account, though the transactions be
ever so numerous ; the effect of which is to lessen the labor of
posting, and to render the process of balancing comparatively
easy — an advantage of no trifling importance.

We cannot, therefore, approve of the practice of those book-
keepers, who, to save themselves the trouble of transcribing the
Cash transactions, post each separate item directly from the
Cash Book to the Ledger. They thus avoid, it is true, the
labor of copying a few folio pages ; but, by giving up the
advantage of combining the different items, they have to post

to the Ledger, during the month, above one hundred entries, instead of perhaps thirty or forty.

The old method of Journalizing and posting each transaction separately — except in very limited concerns, where a Journal may be dispensed with altogether — is both tedious and inconvenient. It unnecessarily swells the accounts with a multiplicity of figures, which greatly increases the difficulty of balancing at the end of the year ; and, to say nothing of labor and loss of time, the liability to error is always in proportion to the number of entries, and *vice versa*. If a hundred sums are posted when one would answer, then a hundred chances of error are incurred where only one was necessary ; and, in the event of an error, a hundred entries must be examined, in many cases, instead of one.

The only way to render the irksome and difficult process of balancing easy, is, to keep the Ledger in such a concise form that it may be considered an index to the Journal, as the Journal is to the Subsidiary Books. "The book-keeper who aims at making the Ledger supply the place of an Account Current Book," says Mr. Booth, after thirty years' experience, " will make himself a slave to no purpose, without ever having the satisfaction of seeing his books kept up ; and, instead of balancing them in two or three days, may spend as many months before it is effected, which I have frequently known to be the case."

The apparent inconvenience of Journalizing *monthly*, occasioned by delay in posting, is amply compensated in the subsequent stages of the work ; and, independently of its other advantages, the Journal becomes to its owner a valuable abstract of his mercantile transactions.

Book-keeping by Double Entry, however familiar to merchants and accountants, appears intricate and difficult to almost every person who has not made it a subject of study and reflection. For the purpose of presenting a synopsis or comprehensive view of the art, we shall here give a practical exemplification of its arrangement and routine, by exhibiting examples of the subordinate books, and also of the manner of classifying entries in the Journal, conformably to modern practice.

The Journal of a mercantile establishment ought to contain, at the beginning of each year, a summary statement of its assets and liabilities,* thus : —

	JANUARY, 1839.		1
Folio of the Ledger.	SUNDRIES *Dr. to Stock,* For the assets and balances in our favor, 31st ult., transferred from Ledger A.		
	Cash,...	10,000	00
	Bills Receivable,..............................	5,000	00
	Merchandise,.................................	8,000	00
	Richard Conder,..............................	1,500	00
	William Simpson,.............................	1,750	00
		26,250	00
	STOCK *Dr. to Sundries,* For the balances against us, 31st ult.		
	To Bills Payable, ...	3,000	00
	To William James,............................	1,200	00
	To James Brown,.............................	800	00
		5,000	00

CASH BOOK. — The Cash Book is perfectly simple in its form and arrangement.   Each folio consists of two pages.   The left-hand page, or *Dr.* side, exhibits a statement of the cash in the merchant's possession at the beginning of the month, and *all* sums received ; and the right-hand page, or *Cr.* side, exhibits a statement of *all* payments or disbursements for the same period. No man can disburse money that he never received : hence it follows that the *Dr.* side of the Cash Book, when correctly kept, can never amount to a less sum than the *Cr.* side.   The difference, if any, between the totals of the two sides, is the balance, or cash in hand.

---

* The several items which constitute the merchant's entire capital, are called his *assets* or *effects ;* and the sums owing by him, his *liabilities* or *debts.* The difference between the effects and debts, at any time, is called his *net* capital or present worth.

The following is an example of the receipts and payments which daily occur in the counting-house : —

Dr.		CASH.				Cr.	1
1839.				1839.			
Jan. 1.	Balance on hand,......	10.000	00	Jan. 2.	By Bills Payable, No. 9,....	500	00
" 5.	To Jas. Kent, on account,..	387	88	" 4.	By James Wilson, paid him,	75	87
" 10.	To Interest from Hume&Co.	13	50	" 8.	By Robert Hall, "	375	00
" 15.	To Jas. Kent,....in full,...	112	12	" 10.	By Hume & Co.,....in full,	1,185	75
" 25.	To Bills Receivable, No. 71,	178	00	" 20.	By Bills Payable, No. 10,...	250	25
" 30.	To Interest,...dividend,...	150	00	" "	By J. Wilson, paid him,....	1,000	00
" "	To Bills Receivable, No. 72,	500	00	" 31.	By R. Hall,.....in full,....	410	00
					Balance to Feb........	7.544	63
		11,341	50			11,341	50

The manner of Journalizing the Cash Book is as follows : —

	JANUARY, 1839.			1
In this column is entered the folio of the Ledger to which the items are transferred.	CASH *Dr. to Sundries,*			
	Received this month, ℣ Cash Book.			
	To James Kent,.......... 5th,......... 387 88			
	15th,......... 112 12	500	00	
	To Interest,.............10th,......... 13 50			
	30th,......... 150 00	163	50	
	To Bills Receivable,.......25th,......... 178 00			
	30th,......... 500 00	678	00	
		1,341	50	
	SUNDRIES *Dr. to Cash,*			
	Paid this month, ℣ Cash Book.			
	Bills Payable,............. 2d,......... 500 00			
	20th,......... 250 25	750	25	
	James Wilson, ... 4th,......... 75 87			
	20th,......... 1,000 00	1,075	87	
	Robert Hall, ... 8th,......... 375 00			
	31st,......... 410 00	785	00	
	Hume & Co.............10th,....................	1,185	75	
		3,796	87	

The above exemplification will serve to convey an idea of the facilities afforded by *monthly* Journalizing. In the first collective entry, 'CASH' is made debtor to sundry accounts for all the money received ; and in the second, sundry accounts are made debtor to 'CASH' for all payments during the month. On comparing the Cash Book with the Journal, it will be seen that the several receipts and payments for each separate account are comprised in one entry ; so that, if there were fifty sums received at different dates, and as many distinct payments, on any *one* account in the same month, it would require only two postings to the Ledger ; and if there were five hundred receipts and payments, they would all be comprehended in two lines in the 'Cash' account.

BILL BOOK. — The Bill Book is ruled with columns for the different details, such as, the number of the bill ; on whose account ; when received or accepted ; the date, and term of payment ; on whom drawn, or to whom granted ; when due ; the amount ; and the event — that is, whether paid or discounted, &c. — thus : —

					BILLS RECEIVABLE.				
No.	When received.	On account of	Drawn by	Date.	Term.	Drawn on	When due.	Amount.
	1839.			1839.			1839.	
1	March 8.	J. Bailey.	W. Adams.	March 1.	60 days.	T. Jones.	May 1-4.	$ 587 78
2	" 10.	T.Watson.	J. Jones.	" 3.	30 "	J. Adams.	April 3-6.	325 00
3	" 12.	J. Bailey.	R. James.	" 5.	90 "	D. Hill.	June 5-8.	240 55

				BILLS PAYABLE.				
No.	Drawn by	Date.	To order of	On account of	Term.	When accepted.	When due.	Amount.
		1839.				1839.	1839.	
1	J. Allen.	March 10.	J. Jones.	J. Allen.	90 days' sight.	March 12.	June 10-13.	235 25
2	Chas. Fox.	" 7.	J. Brown.	C. Fox.	15 " date.	" 14.	March 22-25.	145 75
3	J. Clark.	" 5.	H. Clay.	J. Clark.	30 days.	" 16.	April 5-8.	341 25

. For the convenience of printing, several columns, which are used in business, are omitted in the above examples.

It is customary to keep a distinct register of both Bills

Receivable and Bills Payable in the same book. The Journal entries for the preceding bills are as follows : —

MARCH, 1839.		1
BILLS RECEIVABLE *Dr. to Sundries,* Received this month, ℙ Bill Book.		
To James Bailey, ... 8th,......No. 1,.....587 78		
12th,......No. 3,.....240 55	828	33
To T. Watson,.........10th,......No. 2,..........	325	00
	1,153	33
SUNDRIES *Dr. to Bills Payable,* Accepted this month, ℙ Bill Book.		
James Allen, ...12th,....No. 1,.............	235	25
Charles Fox,...........14th,....No. 2,.............	145	75
James Clark, ...16th,....No. 3,.............	341	25
	722	25

(Ledger folio.)

Inland bills are divided into two sorts, — Drafts or Acceptances, and Promissory Notes, — the former containing an order, the latter a promise, both being of equal obligation. Most mercantile payments are made in drafts, promissory notes, or bills of exchange, which pass from hand to hand till due, like any other circulating medium. They are assignable and indorsable, and, in all respects, nearly assimilated.

———

INVOICE BOOK. — In former times, it was the practice to fold the Invoices in a uniform size, and, after writing on the back the name of the seller, date, &c., to put them away in bundles. But, whenever the purchases are extensive and numerous, the better mode is to paste them into a blank book made of cartridge paper. This book should have its pages numbered, and an index, with columns for dollars and cents. Arrange the Invoices, or Bills of Parcels, one under the other, in regular order, and place the totals in the column ruled for that purpose,

taking care that each amount is placed opposite to its respective
bill.   The following will serve as a specimen : —

NEW YORK, *March* 1, 1839.		170	00
Messrs. JAMES BROWN & Co.			
Bought of R. Johnson,			
20 ps. fine Linen, ...@ 4 75,.......... 95 00			
15 " " do. ....@ 5 00,.......... 75 00			
170 00			
NEW YORK, *March* 4, 1839.		172	80
Messrs. JAMES BROWN & Co.			
Bought of Robert James,			
2 doz. Youths' Hats,.........@ 24 00,......... 48 00			
2 " Men's do. ....@ 60 00,.........120 00			
4 cases, and packing,........@ 1 20,......... 4 80			
172 80			
NEW YORK, *March* 9, 1839.		268	75
Messrs. JAMES BROWN & Co.			
Bought of R. Johnson,			
11 ps. Linen, 25 yds. ea.—275 yds. @ 75 cts......206 25			
5 " do. 25 " ea.—125 " @ 50 cts...... 62 50			
268 75		611	55

The above purchases are Journalized as follows : —

	MARCH, 1839.			
Ledger folios.	MERCHANDISE *Dr. to Sundries,*			
	Purchased this month, ℈ Invoice Book.			
	To R. Johnson,..............1st,.......... 170 00			
	9th,.......... 268 75		438	75
	To Robert James,..........4th,..................		172	80
			611	55

BOOK OF SHIPMENTS. — Some houses enter the particulars
of the Shipments in the Day Book ; but the practice, in well-

6   D*

regulated establishments, is to keep the Invoice Book Outward as a book of record for Shipments, and to Journalize it *monthly* in the same manner as the Cash or Bill Books.

The following specimen will serve as an exemplification of the general form of Invoices : —

INVOICE *of Goods, shipped by James Brown & Co. in the Venus, John King, Master, for New Orleans, by order of R. Johnson, Merchant there, for his account and risk, and to him consigned.*

R. J. No. 1.	48 ps. Cambric Check, 1,344 yds. @ 40 cts. . 537 60 Trunk, and packing,. 5 25	542	85
2.	51 " Calico Check, 1,428 yds. . @ 25 cts. . 357 00 Trunk, and packing, ... 4 75	361	75
3.	15 " Fine Calico, 360 yds. . . . . @ 40 cts. . 144 00 6 " Cambric Check, 144 yds. . @ 50 cts. . 72 00 20 " Muslin Check, 560 yds. . . @ 30 cts. . 168 00 Trunk, and packing, ... 3 50	387	50
		1,292	10
	CHARGES.		
	Cartage, shipping charges, &c. . . . . 4 03 Commission, 2½ ⅌ cent on $ 1,296,. . . . . 32 40 Insurance, and Policy,. . . . . 27 61 Commission, ½ ⅌ cent on Insurance,. 6 59	70	63
	NEW YORK, *March* 15, 1839.	1,362	73

The Journal entries are as follows : —

	MARCH, 1839.		
Ledger folios.	R. JOHNSON *Dr. to Sundries*, For Goods ⅌ Venus, ⅌ Book Shipments,		
	To Merchandise, ... 15th,.	1,292	10
	To Charges,. . . . . "	4	03
	To Insurance,. . . . . "	27	61
	To Commission,. . . . . "	38	99
		1,362	73

SALES BOOK. — The arrangement of the Sales in extensive commission houses, is similar to that of Cash. The details of each separate and distinct consignment are recorded upon opposite pages, with a preamble over both, setting forth the description of the goods, the name of the party from whom received, &c. The left-hand page contains a statement of all charges attending the sale, such as Insurance, Freight, Duty, and the like, including the agent's commission ; and the right-hand page contains the particulars of the Sales, that is, the quantity, price, the amount, and to whom sold. The difference between the two sides, when the Sales are completed, is the *net proceeds*, due to the consigner.

The following is the usual form in which an Account Sales is rendered : —

ACCOUNT SALES of 200 *pieces Linen, received ℗ Union from Dublin, on account James Forbes, of that place.*		
1839. *Sold to* BARCLAY & CO., *at 4 months,*		
March 9. Linen, No. 1,......20 pieces,......@ 44/.....	110	00
2,......30 ″ ......@ 53/.....	198	75
3,......25 ″ ......@ 48/.....	150	00
4,......17 ″ ......@ 20/.....	110	50
5,......23 ″ ......@ 54/.....	155	25
6,......25 ″ ......@ 44/.....	137	50
7,......60 ″ ......@ 60/.....	450	00
200 pieces.	1,312	00
CHARGES.		
Freight, Custom-House Fees, &c........38 50		
Cartage and Porterage,................. 1 25		
Storage and Advertising,................ 4 75		
44 50		
Commission on $1,312, at 5 ℗ cent,......65 60		
	110	10
To JAMES FORBES, *for net proceeds,*...........	1,201	90
NEW YORK, *March* 11, 1839.		
Errors Excepted,		
A. B.		

There is no necessity that the different items of an Invoice or

Account Sales should be arranged in the books in the same order as in the document transmitted. For example, though an Account Sales be kept by debtor and creditor in the books, yet the document is seldom transmitted to the consigner in this form, the sales being first stated, and the charges deducted at the foot, as above. In the books, the different articles are necessarily entered as they occur ; but in the account as rendered, they are combined and arranged in any way that perspicuity or custom may dictate.

The entries, which arise from adjusting the above sales, are Journalized as follows : —

	MARCH, 1839.		
	BARCLAY & Co. *Dr. to Sales of Consignments,* For 200 ps. Linen, account J. Forbes,..............	1,312	00
	SALES OF CONSIGNMENTS *Dr. to Sundries,* For adjustment of sales Linen ℔ Union.		
	To Charges,...........freight, &c................	44	50
	To Commission, ...on sales,..................	65	60
	To James Forbes,......net proceeds,..............	1,201	90
		1,312	00

Ledger folios.

We have now given an exemplification of the Subsidiary Books commonly made use of in the counting-house of a *general merchant*, and which form the ground-work or materials for the Journal. But particular concerns require a variety of different books, according to the nature of the business in which the parties are engaged.

ACCOUNTS CURRENT. — Accounts Current are rather the result than a constituent part of book-keeping, being written out from the Ledger, with very slight variation or addition.

An Account Current is a statement of the mercantile transactions between two persons, disposed in the form of debtor and creditor, which exhibits the state of their affairs up to any given date.

The term *Dr.* is to indicate that the correspondent is debtor for the sums on the left, and the term *Cr.* to indicate that the correspondent is creditor for the sums on the right.

The difference between an Account Current and any other is, simply, that the former is an account of continuous transactions from one period to another, while other accounts embrace only particular things, of which the Account Current is the general depository. The word *current* is, in this case, used to imply the present state of an account, in its course or continued progression. Accounts Current are generally rendered every six or twelve months; and it is common to charge interest on such sums on the debtor side as fall due prior to the time of making up the account, and to allow interest on such sums on the creditor side as are payable prior to the time of making up the account. The following is an example: —

Dr. JAMES THOMPSON, Esq., *New Orleans, in Account Current with A. B., New York.* Cr.						
1839.				1839.		
June 30.	To Balance of ac't. rendered,	325	26	Aug. 15.	By net proceeds of Cotton, ⅌ Cuba, due Sept. 15,..... 875	50
July 14.	To Goods, ⅌ invoice,.......	750	33	Sept. 30.	By proceeds of Sugar, ⅌ Lou-	
" 23.	To Cash, ⅌ receipt,........	325	00		isa, due Oct. 15,.......... 578	25
Oct. 12.	To Goods, ⅌ invoice,.......	150	45	Dec. 31.	By Balance, carried to new	
" 18.	To your Draft paid Hill,.....	125	00		account, ... 223	79
Dec. 31.	To Postage to date,.........	1	50		1,677	54
		1,677	54			
	NEW YORK, *Dec.* 31, 1839.				Errors excepted, A. B.	

CHAPTER V.

FOR the purpose of *initiating* the learner into the practical details of the art, we have given, in the present chapter, a series of transactions of a simple nature, which are placed on the left-hand page ; and the Journal entries for each are seen on the opposite or right-hand page. In these preliminary exercises, the several transactions are Journalized *singly*, as affording the most obvious illustration of the manner of arranging the Journal entries ; but, however excellent as an *initiatory* process, this method is by no means recommended as being applicable to real business.

DIRECTIONS FOR THE LEARNER

First copy the following ' *Transactions*' into a suitable book, leaving the right-hand page blank for the ' *Journal Entries.*' This done, the learner must endeavor to Journalize each transaction according to the best of his skill and knowledge ; and, whenever he is at a loss, he should refer to the instructions contained in Chapter III. In the first instance, the entries should be written upon a slate, and examined by the teacher, or compared with the exemplifications in the printed work, and then, if found correct, transcribed upon the page which was left blank for the purpose. The nature and classification of the accounts in the Ledger should be thoroughly understood by the learner,

46

before he attempts to Journalize ; and hence the *Synopsis*, on pages 22, 23, must be diligently and attentively studied in the outset.

QUESTIONS.

When the learner is able to answer the following questions, he will experience no difficulty in Journalizing the most complicated transactions. — See *Synopsis.*

What is the object of ' *Stock* ' account ? What do you enter on the *Cr.* side ? What on the *Dr.* side ? What does the difference between the two sides show, when the *Cr.* is the greater ? What does it show when the *Dr.* side exceeds the *Cr.* ?

What is the object of ' *Profit and Loss* ' account ? What do you enter on the *Dr.* side ? What on the *Cr.* side ? What does the difference between the two sides of ' Profit and Loss ' exhibit ?

What is the object of the general account of ' *Merchandise* ' ? What do you enter on the *Dr.* side of this account ? What on the *Cr.* side ? What is the *balance* ? What does the difference between the two sides show, when the goods are all sold ?

What is the object of the ' *Cash* ' account ? What do you enter on the *Dr.* side ? What on the *Cr.* ? What does the difference between the two sides of ' Cash ' show ?

What do you mean by ' *Bills Receivable* ' ? (See Note, p. 10.) What is the object of this account ? What do you enter on the *Dr.* side ? What on the *Cr.* side ? What does the difference between the two sides show ?

What are ' *Bills Payable* ' ? What is the object of this account ? What is entered on the *Cr.* side ? What on the *Dr.* side ? What does the difference between the two sides show ?

What is the object of *Personal Accounts* ? What is entered on the *Dr.* side ? What on the *Cr.* side ? What does the balance show ?

When goods are consigned, or sent abroad as an adventure, how are such transactions recorded ? When you receive goods to sell on commission, how do you arrange the account ?

What are the subdivisions of ' *Profit and Loss* ' ?

What do you enter on the *Cr.* side of '*Commission*'?   To what account is the result transferred?

What is entered on the *Dr.* side of '*Interest*,' and on the *Cr.* side?

What do you enter in the account entitled '*Charges*'?

———

What account shows the receipts and payments of cash?   Where do you enter the *sales* and purchases of goods?   When you *receive* a bill, to what account does it belong?   When you *accept* a draft, or *issue* a note, where must it be entered?

What is a simple Journal entry?   What do you understand by a compound entry?   What is the meaning of the word *Sundries*, as applied to the Journal entries?

———

The learner should be continually questioned, in this manner, during the whole course of his studies, and made fully to understand the *reasons* — the *why* and *wherefore* of all that he does.

INTRODUCTORY SET.

[TRANSACTIONS.]

1	New York, *January* 1, 1839.		
Cash in hand this day, which constitutes my Net Capital in trade,..	15,000	00
———— 2 ————		
Paid for Stationery, Blank Books, &c., ℔ Cash Book ...	325	38
———— 4 ————		
Bought of Charles Hammond, Goods, ℔ Invoice, amounting to	8,151	25
———— 6 ————		
Sold James Bruce & Co., 15 pieces Broadcloth, ℔ Sales Book,................	957	12
———— 7 ————		
Paid cash for Goods bought this day, ℔ B. P.............	2,125	75
———— 9 ————		
Bought Goods of Hone & Co., for which I gave my Acceptance, at 30 days' date, ...	857	75
———— 12 ————		
Paid for Advertising, Postages, &c., ℔ Cash Book,........	25	18
———— 15 ————		
Sold Goods to James Hill, as ℔ Sales Book. Received in settlement his Bill, at 90 days,....................	785	50
———— 18 ————		
Sold Goods for cash, ℔ Cash Book,....................	280	31
———— 19 ————		
Accepted Charles Hammond's Draft favor of Smith & Co., at 90 days' date, ...	4,000	00

[JOURNAL ENTRIES.]

	JANUARY 1, 1839.		**1**
$\frac{3}{1}$	CASH *Dr. to Stock,* For Net Capital,.....................................	15,000	00
	──────── 2 ────────		
$\frac{1}{3}$	CHARGES *Dr. to Cash,* For Stationery, &c.............................	325	38
	──────── 4 ────────		
$\frac{2}{4}$	MERCHANDISE *Dr. to C. Hammond,* Purchased, ℗ Invoice,...........................	8,151	25
	──────── 6 ────────		
$\frac{4}{2}$	J. BRUCE & Co. *Dr. to Merchandise,* For 15 pieces Broadcloth, ℗ B. P.................	957	12
	──────── 7 ────────		
$\frac{2}{3}$	MERCHANDISE *Dr. to Cash,* Purchased this day, ℗ B. P......................	2,125	75
	──────── 9 ────────		
$\frac{2}{3}$	MERCHANDISE *Dr. to Bills Payable,* For Acceptance favor Hone & Co.................	857	75
	──────── 12 ────────		
$\frac{1}{3}$	CHARGES *Dr. to Cash,* For Advertising, Postages, &c....................	25	18
	──────── 15 ────────		
$\frac{3}{2}$	BILLS RECEIVABLE *Dr. to Merchandise,* For J. Hill's Note, at 90 days' date,...............	785	50
	──────── 18 ────────		
$\frac{3}{2}$	CASH *Dr. to Merchandise,* For sales this day,...............................	280	31
	──────── 19 ────────		
$\frac{4}{3}$	C. HAMMOND *Dr. to Bills Payable,* Accepted his Draft, at 90 days' date, for...........	4,000	00

[TRANSACTIONS.]

2	NEW YORK, *January* 25, 1839.		
I have drawn on J. Bruce & Co., at 10 days' sight, for amount of purchase 6th inst......................		957	12
———— 28 ————			
Sold Goods to James Brown & Son, and received in payment their Note, at 90 days,............600 00 Cash for the balance,........................600 00		1,200	00
———— 29 ————			
Paid Charles Hammond, ⅌ Receipt, Cash in full,.....................................		4,151	25
———— 80 ————			
Sold James Bruce & Co. Goods, ⅌ Sales Book,.............................		989	75
———— " ————			
Paid Postages, &c., this month, ⅌ Cash Book, ...		15	78
———— FEBRUARY 1, 1839. ————			
Bought of Charles Hammond, Goods, ⅌ Bill Parcels,.............................		583	40
———— 4 ————			
Sold Goods this day, ⅌ Sales Book, viz. to James Peters,..................................... Rufus Dean,.. Henry Pope, ...		350 575 829	22 88 75
		1,755	85
———— 6 ————			
Received Cash for Bruce & Co.'s Acceptance, ⅌ Cash Book,		957	12

<table>
<tr><td colspan="2" align="center">JANUARY 25, 1839.</td><td align="right">2</td><td></td></tr>
<tr><td>3
—
4</td><td>BILLS RECEIVABLE Dr. to J. Bruce & Co.
For my Draft on them, at 10 days' sight, ...</td><td>957</td><td>12</td></tr>
<tr><td colspan="2" align="center">——————— 28 ———————</td><td></td><td></td></tr>
<tr><td>2

3
3</td><td>SUNDRIES Dr. to Merchandise,
Sold J. Brown & Son, ℘ S. B.
Bills Receivable,..........℘ B. B.................
Cash, ...℘ C. B.................</td><td>600
600
——
1,200</td><td>00
00
——
00</td></tr>
<tr><td colspan="2" align="center">——————— 29 ———————</td><td></td><td></td></tr>
<tr><td>4
—
3</td><td>CHARLES HAMMOND Dr. to Cash,
Paid him in full,.............................</td><td>4,151</td><td>25</td></tr>
<tr><td colspan="2" align="center">——————— 30 ———————</td><td></td><td></td></tr>
<tr><td>4
—
2</td><td>JAMES BRUCE & Co. Dr. to Merchandise,
Sold them, ℘ S. B.............................</td><td>989</td><td>75</td></tr>
<tr><td colspan="2" align="center">——————— '' ———————</td><td></td><td></td></tr>
<tr><td>1
—
3</td><td>CHARGES Dr. to Cash,
Paid Postages, &c...........................</td><td>15</td><td>78</td></tr>
<tr><td colspan="2" align="center">——————— FEBRUARY 1, 1839. ———————</td><td></td><td></td></tr>
<tr><td>2
—
4</td><td>MERCHANDISE Dr. to C. Hammond,
Purchased this day, ℘ B. P....................</td><td>583</td><td>40</td></tr>
<tr><td colspan="2" align="center">——————— 4 ———————</td><td></td><td></td></tr>
<tr><td>2

4
4
5</td><td>SUNDRIES Dr. to Merchandise,
For sales this day.
James Peters, ...℘ B. P.................
Rufus Dean,........... '' ....
Henry Pope,........... '' ....</td><td>350
575
829
——
1,755</td><td>22
88
75
——
85</td></tr>
<tr><td colspan="2" align="center">——————— 6 ———————</td><td></td><td></td></tr>
<tr><td>3
—
3</td><td>CASH Dr. to Bills Receivable,
Rec^d for Bruce & Co.'s Acceptance,.............</td><td>957</td><td>12</td></tr>
</table>

E *

[TRANSACTIONS.]

3	NEW YORK, *February* 8, 1839.		
Received the following Bills, dated the 4th inst., at 30 days, ₣ B. B., viz.			
James Peters's, ...		350	22
Rufus Dean's, ...		575	88
Henry Pope's, ...		829	75
		1,755	85
———— 10 ————			
Bought Goods as follows, ₣ Invoice Book, viz. of			
Charles Hammond, ...		387	97
Buchanan & Co...............................		78	25
James Finlay & Co...........................		51	75
		517	97
———— " ————			
Paid Postage, Cartage, &c., ₣ Cash Book,..............		8	25
———— " ————			
The Bank of Commerce has discounted Henry Pope's Note, due March 8,			
Cash received,............................826 20			
Discount allowed,........................ 3 55			
		829	75
———— " ————			
Transferred to C. Hammond, J. Hill's Note, due April 18,..		785	50
———— " ————			
Paid my Acceptance favor of Hone & Co., due this day, ₣ Cash Book,....................................		857	75
———— 25 ————			
Bought Goods of Simpson & Co., ₣ Invoice ; gave them in settlement my			
Note,...........at 60 days,...........1,000 00			
Cash,...........for balance, ... *800 00*		1,800	00

[JOURNAL ENTRIES.]

				3
	FEBRUARY 8, 1839.			
3	BILLS RECEIVABLE *Dr. to Sundries,*			
	For Bills received this day, ℔ B. B.			
4	To James Peters........................	350	22	
4	To Rufus Dean,.........................	575	88	
5	To Henry Pope,....	829	75	
		1,755	85	
	——————— 10 ———————			
2	MERCHANDISE *Dr. to Sundries,*			
	For Purchases this day,			
4	To Charles Hammond, ...	387	97	
4	To Buchanan & Co.....................	78	25	
5	To James Finlay & Co.................	51	75	
		517	97	
1/3	——————— " ———————			
	CHARGES *Dr. to Cash,*			
	For Postage, &c......................	8	25	
	——————— " ———————			
3	SUNDRIES *Dr. to Bills Receivable,*			
	For Pope's Note, discounted at the Bank of Commerce,			
3	Cash,................................	826	20	
1	Profit and Loss,.....................	3	55	
		829	75	
4/3	——————— " ———————			
	C. HAMMOND *Dr. to Bills Receivable,*			
	For Hill's Note, transferred,........	785	50	
3/3	——————— " ———————			
	BILLS PAYABLE *Dr. to Cash,*			
	Paid Acceptance to Hone & Co.........	857	75	
	——————— 25 ———————			
2	MERCHANDISE *Dr. to Sundries,*			
	Purchased this day,			
3	To Bills Payable,....................	1,000	00	
3	To Cash, ...	800	00	
		1,800	00	

[TRANSACTIONS.]

4		
New York, *February* 28, 1839.		
Sold James Bruce & Co.		
Goods, ℀ Sales Book,............................	1,579	23
—————— " ——————		
Paid charges on shipment, &c., ℀ Cash Book,...........	58	97
—————— March 1, 1839. ——————		
Effected Insurance with the Globe Insurance Co. on Goods shipped ℀ Jane for New Orleans.		
Gave my note for Premium and Policy,..................	27	14
—————— " ——————		
Shipped ℀ Jane for, New Orleans, on account and risk of J. Dana & Co., ℀ Invoice Book,		
Goods, ...amounting to..............	975	84
Charges,..............at shipping,...............	31	42
Insurance, ...as above,..................	27	14
Commission, ...on Insurance, ...	5	52
	1,039	92
—————— 2 ——————		
Insured with Hope Insurance Co., account of George Smith, $3,240 00, on 15 hhds. Sugar and 20 bales Cotton, consigned ℀ the Ann.		
Paid Premium and Policy in cash,..................77 28		
Commission,....................................16 20	93	48
—————— 3 ——————		
Received James Bruce & Co.'s Acceptance, at 30 days' date,	989	75
—————— 4 ——————		
Paid charges on Produce consigned ℀ the Ann, in cash,...	220	27
—————— 5 ——————		
Sold James Peters,		
20 bales Cotton, ℀ Ann,.......(Smith's Sales,).......	896	75

[JOURNAL ENTRIES.]

			4
	FEBRUARY 28, 1839.		
$\frac{4}{2}$	JAMES BRUCE & Co. *Dr. to Merchandise,*		
	₱ Sales Book,...............................	1,579	23
	"		
$\frac{1}{3}$	CHARGES *Dr. to Cash,*		
	Paid on shipment, &c.........................	58	97
	MARCH 1, 1839.		
$\frac{2}{3}$	INSURANCE *Dr. to Bills Payable,*		
	For Note to Globe Insurance Co...................	27	14
	"		
5	J. DANA & Co. *Dr. to Sundries,*		
	For Invoice ₱ Jane,		
2	To Merchandise,..............................	975	84
1	To Charges,..................................	31	42
2	To Insurance,................................	27	14
2	To Commission,..............................	5	52
		1 039	92
5	GEORGE SMITH *Dr. to Sundries,*		
	For Insurance on Produce ₱ Ann,		
3	To Cash,.....................................	77	28
2	To Commission,..............................	16	20
		93	48
	3		
$\frac{3}{4}$	BILLS RECEIVABLE *Dr. to James Bruce & Co.*		
	For Acceptance, at 30 days, ...	989	75
	4		
$\frac{1}{3}$	CHARGES *Dr. to Cash,*		
	On Produce, ₱ Ann, ...	220	27
	5		
$\frac{4}{2}$	JAMES PETERS *Dr. to Smith's Sales,*		
	For 20 bales Cotton, ₱ Ann,...................	896	75

8

[TRANSACTIONS.]

5			
New York, *March 7, 1839.*			
Paid Buchanan & Co.			
Cash in full, ℘ C. B............................		78	25
─────────── 8 ───────────		—	—
Allowed James Bruce & Co. 2 ℘ cent discount on $1,579,..		31	58
─────────── 12 ───────────			
Rendered Account Sales of 20 bales Cotton, ℘ Ann, ℘ S. B.			
and debited *Smith's Sales* as follows : —			
To Charges............for freight, &c...........		85	30
To Commission.........on sales,................		35	87
To George Smith,.....*for net proceeds,*..........		775	58
		896	75
─────────── 15 ───────────			
J. Dana & Co. have accepted my Draft, at 90 days' date,...		1,039	92
─────────── 17 ───────────			
Effected with the Globe Insurance Co. insurance on $2,800			
on Goods ℘ Nero, for New Orleans.			
Paid Premium and Policy, *cash*, ...		61	34
─────────── 18 ───────────			
Paid charges on shipments, &c. ℘ Cash Book,............		85	39
─────────── 19 ───────────			
Shipped ℘ Nero, on account George Smith, New Orleans,			
℘ Book Shipments,			
Goods,............℘ Invoice, ...		2,550	30
Charges,...........at shipping,.................		75	37
Insurance,..........as above,...................		61	34
Commission,......................................		72	87
		2,759	88
─────────── 21 ───────────			
Sold Buchanan & Co.			
15 hhds. Sugar, ℘ Ann, ℘ S. B.....(Smith's Sales,)....		3,360	25

[JOURNAL ENTRIES.]

	MARCH 7, 1839.		5
$\frac{5}{3}$	BUCHANAN & Co. *Dr. to Cash,*		
	Paid them in full,...............................	78	25
	———————— 8 ————————		
$\frac{1}{4}$	PROFIT AND LOSS *Dr. to James Bruce & Co.*		
	For Discount allowed,...........................	31	58
	———————— 12 ————————		
2	SMITH'S SALES *Dr. to Sundries,*		
	For adjustment of sales Cotton, ℔ Ann, ℔ S. B.		
1	To Charges, ...	85	30
2	To Commission, ...	35	87
5	To George Smith,.............................	775	58
		896	75
	———————— 15 ————————		
$\frac{3}{5}$	BILLS RECEIVABLE *Dr. to J. Dana & Co.*		
	For their Acceptance, at 90 days,................	1,039	92
	———————— 17 ————————		
$\frac{2}{3}$	INSURANCE *Dr. to Cash,*		
	On Goods ℔ Nero, ...	61	34
	———————— 18 ————————		
$\frac{1}{3}$	CHARGES *Dr. to Cash,*		
	Paid charges on Shipments,......................	85	39
	———————— 19 ————————		
5	GEORGE SMITH *Dr. to Sundries,*		
	For Goods ℔ Nero, ℔ order,		
2	To Merchandise, ...	2,550	30
1	To Charges, ...	75	37
2	To Insurance, ...	61	34
2	To Commission, ...	72	87
		2,759	88
	———————— 21 ————————		
$\frac{5}{2}$	BUCHANAN & Co. *Dr. to Smith's Sales,*		
	For 15 hhds. Sugar, ℔ Ann,.....................	3,360	25

[TRANSACTIONS.]

6	New York, *March* 25, 1839.		
Paid my Note in favor of Globe Insurance Co............		27	14
"			
Paid James Finlay & Co. Cash, ℔ C. B..................................		51	75
"			
Paid charges on Produce consigned ℔ Ann,.............		45	78
"			
Made up Account Sales of 15 hhds. Sugar, ℔ Ann, ℔ S. B., and debited *Smith's Sales* as follows : —			
To Charges, ...for freight, &c............		180	75
To Commission, ...on sales,................		134	41
To George Smith,....*for net proceeds,*..........		3,045	9
		3,360	25
31			
Paid cash for Store-rent, and Clerk's salary,.............		450	00

[JOURNAL ENTRIES.]

	MARCH 25, 1839.		6
$\frac{3}{3}$	BILLS PAYABLE *Dr. to Cash,* Paid Note favor Globe Insurance Co................	27	14
$\frac{5}{3}$	" J. FINLAY & Co. *Dr. to Cash,* Paid them,.....................................	51	75
$\frac{1}{3}$	" CHARGES *Dr. to Cash,* On Produce ℔ Ann,.............................	45	78
2 1 ·2 5	" SMITH'S SALES *Dr. to Sundries,* For adjustment of sales 15 hhds. Sugar, ℔ Ann, To Charges,.................................. To Commission,.............................. To George Smith,............................	180 134 3,045 3,360	75 41 09 25
$\frac{1}{3}$	31 CHARGES *Dr. to Cash,* Rent and Clerk's salary,......................	450	00

Mem. — The goods on hand 31st March, are valued at $5,786. This item constitutes the *balance* of 'Merchandise' account, in making a statement of the merchant's assets and liabilities at this date. (See Remarks, page 70.)

F

CHAPTER VI.

DIRECTIONS FOR POSTING AND BALANCING THE LEDGER.

A STATEMENT of all the facts relative to any person or thing, by which the capital of a concern has been affected, is technically called an *account*.

To open an account, signifies to enter its title for the first time in the Ledger; after which, the respective items belonging to it are transferred from the Journal or subordinate books, as often as may be convenient. This is called *posting*. Hence, to post an article is to place it to its appropriate account. The principal object of the Journal is to facilitate this process of posting, and to abridge the Ledger entries.

The distribution or classification of accounts is perfectly arbitrary, in the first instance. They may be opened promiscuously, or, which is preferable, similar accounts may be placed contiguous to each other. Thus 'Stock,' 'Profit and Loss,' 'Commission,' 'Charges,' 'Interest,' and the like, may form one general division; and 'Cash,' 'Bills Receivable,' 'Bills Payable,' and the Personal Accounts, another.

As soon as an account is opened, the title, and page of the Ledger where it is found, must be entered in an Index appropriated to that object. The following exemplifications will afford a sufficient illustration of the process of transferring the items which compose the accounts from the Journal to the Ledger.

DIRECTIONS FOR POSTING.

1. — When the Journal entry consists of but one debit and one credit item. For example : —

	JANUARY 1, 1839.		1
*2 — 1	CASH *Dr. to Stock,* For capital in trade, ...	15,000	00

By the help of the Index, turn to the 'Cash' account, and on the left-hand or *Dr.* side write ' *To Stock*, $15,000.' Place the date and page of the Journal in the proper columns. Then turn to the 'Stock' account, and on the right-hand or *Cr.* side write ' *By Cash*, $15,000,' prefixing the date, &c., as before — thus : —

Dr.			STOCK.			*Cr.*	1
			1839. Jan. 1.	By Cash,............	1	15,000	00

Dr.			CASH.			*Cr.*	2
1839. Jan. 1.	To Stock,..........	1	15,000	00			

* The figures in these columns refer to the page of the *Ledger*, and those in the Ledger refer back to the page of the *Journal*.

2. — When the Journal entry contains but one debit and several credit items. For example : —

				1
	FEBRUARY 10, 1839.			
1	MERCHANDISE *Dr. to Sundries,* For purchases this day,			
2	To Charles Hammond,..		387	97
3	To Buchanan & Co..		78	25
4	To James Finlay & Co..		57	75
			517	97

Turn to the account of ' Merchandise,' and on the left-hand side write ' *To Sundries*' for the total, $517 97; and credit each person ' *By Merchandise*' for his respective share — thus : —

Dr.	MERCHANDISE.				Cr.		1
1839. Feb. 10.	To Sundries,........	1	517	97			

Dr.	CHARLES HAMMOND.				Cr.		2
				1839. Feb. 10.	By Merchandise,......	1	387	97

Dr.	BUCHANAN & CO.				Cr.		3
				1839. Feb. 10.	By Merchandise,.....	1	78	25

Dr.	JAMES FINLAY & CO.				Cr.		4
				1839. Feb. 10.	By Merchandise,.....	1	57	75

3 — When the Journal entry consists of several debit items, and but one credit item. For example : —

FEBRUARY 4, 1839.		2	
1	Sundries *Dr. to Merchandise,* For sales this day,		
5	James Peters,...	350	22
6	Rufus Dean,...	575	88
7	Henry Pope,...	829	75
		1,755	85

Turn to 'Merchandise,' as before, and on the *Cr.* side write '*By Sundries,* $1,755 85;' then debit each personal account '*To Merchandise*' for its respective sum ; prefix dates, and be particular to insert the Journal page *from* which the entry is transferred, and also, in the Journal, the Ledger page *to* which the entry is transferred, so as to afford a ready reference from one book to another — thus : —

Dr.	MERCHANDISE.				*Cr.*	1	
				1839. Feb. 4.	By Sundries,...... 2	1,755	85

Dr.	JAMES PETERS.		*Cr.*	5	
1839. Feb. 4.	To Merchandise,..	2	350	22	

Dr.	RUFUS DEAN.		*Cr.*	6	
1839. Feb. 4.	To Merchandise,..	2	575	88	

Dr.	HENRY POPE.		*Cr.*	7	
1839. Feb. 4.	To Merchandise,..	2	829	75	

4. — When the Journal entry is composed of several debit and several credit items. (See page 33.)

Turn to each account which is to be debited, and on the left-hand side write ' *To Sundries ;* ' and then turn to each account which is to be credited, and on the right-hand side say ' *By Sundries* ' for their respective sums.

Having finished posting, it will be expedient, before you balance the Ledger, to ascertain if the amounts of the debtor and creditor sides correspond. For this purpose, prepare a sheet of paper as follows : —

Drs.	TRIAL BALANCE.	*Crs.*
	(Titles of the Accounts.)	

Write the titles in the centre, and place the sum of the debtor side of each account in the left, and the sum of the creditor side in the right-hand column ; add the columns, and, if the Ledger is correct, the amounts will agree.

The principle of the 'Trial Balance' is that, in every Journal entry, the *Drs.* equal the *Crs.* ; and it is obvious, if the respective sums were correctly placed, that the aggregate amount of the *Dr.* side of the Ledger will be equal to that of the *Cr.* side. If otherwise, some mistake has been committed. The apparent difference may not exceed a few dollars or cents ; still the smallest discrepancy shows the existence of error, and to an extent, perhaps, greatly beyond the fraction in question. It often happens that, as the examination proceeds, the difference undergoes a change from a smaller to a larger amount, without increasing the difficulty of discovering the error, which is as likely to have occurred in the case of a large as a small sum. Differences, when in round numbers, such as $10, $100, $1,000, generally lie in the *addition* ; fractional sums frequently in the posting. All this, however, is uncertain. Hence the necessity of examining the whole ; and young book-keepers are often obliged to pass week after week in the tedious labor of revising, adding, and subtracting, in order to bring their accounts to a balance.

The only effectual means of lessening the labor and perplexity of this operation is, to limit the number of entries ; in other words, by combining and classifying the transactions in the Journal, to comprise as much as possible in those aggregate amounts which are transferred to the Ledger, and to exercise great care in every stage of the work.

The following are the most usual mistakes in posting which *do not* affect the Trial Balance, viz.

1. A sum entered to a wrong account, but on the same side of the Ledger as that to which it belongs.

2. A Journal entry wholly omitted.

3. A Journal entry twice posted.

The most effectual check against the above, or any similar mistakes, is a comparison of the books by *two* persons. One has the Journal, and reads the Ledger folio, the title of the account, and the *Drs.* and *Crs.* ; while the other turns to the account in the Ledger, and marks off the entry with a dot, if correct. When all the accounts have been thus examined, glance over the Ledger to observe if the mark of comparison be. affixed to each entry. If not, turn to the entry in the Journal which had not been marked, and see if it is right.

The Ledger should be kept in the most concise form. The insertions ought never to exceed a line each, or to contain more than the *title* of the Journal entry to which they refer. To a person unacquainted with book-keeping, this brevity is apt to be considered unsatisfactory ; and it was formerly the practice to add, in each line, a few explanatory words : this is still done in some counting-houses; but such explanations are practicable only in a limited business. Whenever the transactions are numerous and varied, all particulars should be left out of the Ledger, for two reasons : they increase the labor of the book-keeper, and they never can be so full or circumstantial as to supersede the necessity of an Account Current Book.

When the space allotted for an account is filled up, the amount must be transferred to another folio. For this purpose, add both sides, and write opposite to the amounts, ' *Transferred to fol.* —.' Then, after entering the new *folio* in the index, and opening the account anew, write on the *Dr.* side, ' *To amount from fol.* —,' inserting the *folio* where the account was first opened. The sums should be left blank, or inserted with a black lead pencil till the books are compared, as an error in any of the entries will occasion an alteration in the amount. When either side of an account is full, both sides should be transferred, and a diagonal line drawn to fill up the vacant space on the side which requires it.

GENERAL BALANCE.

In every well-regulated establishment, the several accounts are adjusted at least once a year. This process is called *balancing ;* the design of which is to collect the balances or assets of the concern into a concise abstract, to ascertain the profit or loss, and to exhibit the present state of the capital or stock.

The *Balance* of an account is the difference between its two sides, and forms a constituent part of your *Effects* or *Debts ;* for, whenever this difference in any account is neither effects nor debts, it belongs to ' *Profit and Loss,*' and must be transferred accordingly.

When an account is added, the two sides will be equal without further entry, or may be made equal by entering the difference on the smaller side. In the former case, the account is said to be *closed*; in the latter, it is merely *equilibrated*, but continues open. For example : —

Dr.			A . B .		Cr.	
1839			1839			
Jan. 1	To Merchandise, ...	100 00	Jan. 15	By Cash,............. ...	100	00
" 19	To .....do............	355 00	Feb. 10	By do.	300	00
" 30	To .....do............	145 00	" 28	By do.	200	00
		600 00			600	00

In this instance, both sides, when added, are equal, and therefore the account is *closed*. The following is an exemplification of the second case : —

Dr.			C . D .		Cr.	
1839			1839			
Jan. 1	To Merchandise, ...	300 00	Jan. 15	By Cash................	180	00
" 31	To .....do............	150 00	June 30	*By Balance,*............	500	00
Feb. 15	To .....do............	230 00				
		680 00			680	00

The *Dr.* side of C. D.'s account amounts to $680, and the *Cr.* side is only $180. Hence, to *equilibrate* it, subtract the smaller sum from the greater : the difference is $500, which place in that column whose total is least, with the words ' *By Balance* ' before it; and thus both sides *are made* equal. This is called *balancing* an account.

In balancing the Ledger for the purpose of making a statement of the assets and liabilities of the concern, the several accounts are adjusted as follows : —

1. ' Cash,' ' Bills Receivable,' ' Bills Payable,' and the Personal Accounts, are closed *To* or *By Balance*. In all these accounts, the *difference* between the two sides is either effects

or debts ; and hence they are equilibrated by placing this difference on the smaller side, with the words *To* or *By Balance*,
as the case may require.

2. '*Merchandise,*' or any similar account, opened with a view
to show gain or loss on particular departments of the business, is
closed differently.

The learner must pay particular attention to the manner of
adjusting this class of accounts. For instance : 'Merchandise'
contains on the debtor side the outlay for goods, and on the
creditor side the returns ; the sales being completed, the *difference* is gain or loss. But if only a *part* of the property has been
disposed of, the difference between the two sides is devoid of
meaning ; that is, it shows neither the balance of the account
nor the gain or loss resulting from it. In all such cases, the
value unsold constitutes the *balance,* and must be entered on the
Cr. side ; the difference is then the gain or loss *on the quantity
sold.*

This balance, of course, forms a part of the merchant's *effects,*
and is entered, with all other items in his favor, on the *Dr.* side
of the 'Balance Sheet.' Suppose, for illustration, that the *Dr.*
side of 'Merchandise,' when added, amounts to $20,000, and
the *Cr.* side to $15,000 ; and that, on taking an inventory, the
quantity on hand is estimated at $7,500. In this case, to adjust
the account, we enter the goods unsold on the *Cr.* side ; the
returns are then complete, from which deduct the whole outlay,
and the difference is the *gain* on the quantity sold. Thus : —

Dr.			MERCHANDISE.		Cr.	
Amount of purchases,.........	20,000	00	Amount of sales,..............	15,000	00
Difference, *gain,**.............	2,500	00	*Balance** on hand,.............	7,500	00
	22,500	00		22,500	00
* The *gain* is transferred to the 'Profit and Loss ' account.			* This forms a part of your *effects,* and must be entered in the ' Balance ' account.			

In order to render this process as simple as the nature of the thing admits, we will present another view of the subject. The purchases amount to $20,000, and the sales to $15,000. Now, it is obvious that the difference between the actual cost *of the quantity sold* and the sales is the gain. To arrive at this result, we might *deduct* the value on hand from the amount purchased, and that product from the sales, thus : —

1. — The purchases are......20,000	2. — Amount of sales,......15,000
Deduct am' on hand, ... 7,500	Cost, deducted,........12,500
Estimated cost,.........12,500	*Gain*, as before, ... 2,500

The two operations, it will be perceived, are, in principle, essentially the same ; but one may serve to illustrate the other.

All accounts of a like nature — such as ships, houses, lands, funded property, shipments or adventures — are adjusted in a similar manner. The present value of the property unsold is the *balance* of the account, and, when entered on the *Cr.* side, the difference is gain or loss. When no returns have been made, the total of the *Dr.* side is the balance.

At every general balance, *transfer* the difference or result of ' *Charges*,' ' *Commission*,' ' *Interest*,' &c., to the proper side of ' *Profit and Loss.*'

Having ascertained, by means of the ' Trial Balance,' that the Ledger has been correctly posted, or, at least, that the amounts of both sides agree, to adjust the accounts, proceed in the following manner : —

Prepare two sheets of paper, ruled with money columns, in the form of *Dr.* and *Cr.* ; write ' Profit and Loss Sheet' as the title of one, and ' Balance Sheet' as the title of the other, thus : —

Dr.	PROFIT AND LOSS SHEET.				*Cr.*
Enter on this side every item of *loss*, including the amount already posted to the *debit* of ' Profit and Loss ' in the Ledger.			Enter on this side every item *of gain*, including the amount already posted to the *credit* of ' Profit and Loss ' in the Ledger.		

The sheet of paper which exhibits a clear and distinct abstract of the merchant's assets and liabilities is called the 'Balance Sheet;' thus : —

Dr.	B A L A N C E S H E E T .	*Cr.*
In the left-hand money column enter the *assets*, or balances in your favor.		In the right-hand money column enter the *liabilities*, or balances against you.

The assets of a concern, deducting its liabilities, can be nothing more than the original capital, increased by the gains, or decreased by the losses.

When you have entered all the gains and losses in the 'Profit and Loss Sheet,' add the two columns, and subtract one from the other : the difference is the net gain or loss, as the case may be.   To this add the net capital at commencing, and the result will be your present worth ; which must correspond, if correct, with the difference between the two sides of the 'Balance Sheet.'

If, for the purpose of transferring each item to its proper place, the particulars of the 'Profit and Loss' and 'Balance sheets are to be inserted in the *Journal,* the following will be the form of the closing entries : —

1. — *For the Profit and Loss Sheet.*

PROFIT AND LOSS *Dr. to* SUNDRIES — namely,
To the several accounts on the *Dr.* side.

SUNDRIES *Dr. to* PROFIT AND LOSS — namely,
The several accounts on the *Cr.* side.

2. — *For the Balance Sheet.*

BALANCE *Dr. to* SUNDRIES — namely,
To the several accounts on the *Dr.* side.

SUNDRIES *Dr. to* BALANCE — namely,
The several accounts on the *Cr.* side.

These entries, when posted into the Ledger, will close all the accounts.

The reason of the *difference* of ' STOCK' agreeing with the *difference* of 'BALANCE' is obvious from the nature of the articles collected. The debtor side of 'Balance' contains the amount of your effects ; the creditor side the sums you owe. The difference shows your capital at the time of balancing.

The debtor side of 'Stock' contained the amount of debts, and the creditor side the amount of effects at commencing. The difference was the net capital ; and, when the gain is added to, or loss deducted from it, the result must also exhibit the present capital.

' *Stock*' and ' *Balance*' accounts, therefore, both point out how much you are worth ; the former from your capital at the beginning, allowance being made for the gain or loss ; the latter from a view of your present effects and debts. Thus the state of your affairs is brought together in a narrow compass, under your view, and the articles of the 'Balance Sheet' supply materials for the first entries in the Journal on commencing the next year

It is not necessary to begin new books after balancing, nor to open the accounts anew, unless the present Ledger be filled up. The balances may be brought down, and the accounts continued in the same folios.

When a person, in the course of business, comes to have several sets of books, it is usual to distinguish them by letters ; as, Ledger A, B, &c.

10   G

INTRODUCTORY SET. — LEDGER.

INDEX.

1

Dr.				STOCK.			Cr.	
1839				1839				
Mar. 31	*To Balance,*	17,191	36	Jan. 1	By Cash, ...	1	15,000	00
				Mar. 31	*By Profit and Loss,*...		2,191	36
		17,191	36				17,191	36

Dr.				PROFIT AND LOSS.			Cr.	
1839				1839				
Feb. 15	To Bills Receivable, .	3	3	55	Mar. 31	By Merchandise, ...	2,823	78
Mar. 8	To J. Bruce & Co....	5	31	58	*" "*	By Commission, ...	264	87
" 31	*To Charges,*		862	16				
" "	To STOCK, ...		2,191	36				
			3,088	65			3,088	65

Dr.				CHARGES.			Cr.	
1839				1839				
Jan. 2	To Cash, ...	1	325	38	Mar. 1	By J. Dana & Co.....	31	42
" 12	To do.	1	25	18	" 12	By Smith's Sales, ...	85	30
" 30	To do.	2	15	78	" 19	By George Smith, ...	75	37
Feb. 11	To do.	3	8	25	" 25	By Smith's Sales, ...	180	75
" 28	To do.	4	58	97	" 31	*By Profit and Loss,* ...	862	16
Mar. 4	To do.	4	220	27				
" 18	To do.	5	85	39				
" 25	To do.	6	45	78				
" 31	To do.	6	450	00				
			1,235	00			1,235	00

G *

2

Dr.	INSURANCE.						Cr.		
1839						1839			
Mar. 1	To Bills Payable,....	4	27	14		Mar. 1	By J. Dana & Co.....	4	27	14
" 17	To Cash,............	5	61	34		" 19	By George Smith,....	5	61	34
			88	48					83	48

Dr.	COMMISSION.						Cr. ·		
1839						1839			
Mar. 31	To Profit and Loss,...		264	87		Mar. 1	By J. Dana & Co.....	4	5	52
						" 2	By George Smith,....	4	16	20
						" 12	By Smith's Sales,....	5	35	87
						" 19	By George Smith,....	5	72	87
						" 25	By Smith's Sales,....	6	134	41
			264	87					264	87

Dr.	MERCHANDISE.						Cr.		
1839						1839			
Jan. 4	To C. Hammond,....	1	8,151	25		Jan. 6	By J. Bruce & Co.....	1	957	12
" 7	To Cash,............	1	2,125	75		" 15	By Bills Receivable,..	1	785	50
" 9	To Bills Payable, ...	1	857	75		" 18	By Cash,............	1	280	31
Feb. 1	To C. Hammond,....	2	583	40		" 28	By Sundries, ...	2	1,200	00
" 10	To Sundries, ...	3	517	97		" 30	By J. Bruce & Co....	2	989	75
" 25	To do.	3	1,800	00		Feb. 4	By Sundries, ...	2	1,755	85
" 31	To Profit and Loss,...		2,823	78		" 28	By J. Bruce & Co....	4	1,579	23
						Mar. 1	By J. Dana & Co.....	4	975	84
						" 19	By George Smith,....	5	2,550	30
						" 31	By Balance,..........		5,786	00
			16,859	90					16,859	90

Dr.	SMITH'S SALES.						Cr.		
1839						1839			
Mar. 12	To Sundries, ...	5	896	75		Mar. 5	By James Peters, ...	4	896	75
" 25	To do.	6	3,360	25		" 21	By Buchanan & Co...	5	3,360	25
			4,257	00					4,257	00

3

Dr.				CASH.				Cr.

1839					1839			
Jan. 1	To Stock,............	1	15,000	00	Jan. 2	By Charges, ...	1	325 38
" 18	To Merchandise,.....	1	280	31	" 7	By Merchandise, ...	1	2,125 75
" 28	To do.	2	600	00	" 12	By Charges...........	1	25 18
Feb. 6	To Bills Receivable,.	2	957	12	" 29	By C. Hammond,....	2	4,151 25
" 15	To do. .	3	826	20	" 30	By Charges, ...	2	15 78
					Feb. 11	By do.	3	8 25
					" 15	By Bills Payable,.....	3	857 75
					" 28	By Merchandise,.....	3	800 00
					" "	By Charges, ...	4	58 97
					Mar. 2	By George Smith,....	4	77 28
					" 4	By Charges, ...	4	220 27
					" 7	By Buchanan & Co...	5	78 25
					" 17	By Insurance,........	5	61 34
					" 18	By Charges, ...	5	85 39
					" 25	By Bills Payable,.....	6	27 14
					" "	By J. Finlay & Co....	6	51 75
					" "	By Charges, ...	6	45 78
					" 31	By do.	6	450 00
					" "	By Balance,..........	6	8,198 12
			17,663	63				17,663 63

Dr.				BILLS RECEIVABLE.				Cr.

1839					1839			
Jan. 15	To Merchandise,.....	1	785	50	Feb. 6	By Cash,............	2	957 12
" 25	To J. Bruce & Co....	2	957	12	" 15	By Sundries..........	3	829 75
" 28	To Merchandise,.....	2	600	00	" "	By C. Hammond,....	3	785 50
Feb. 8	To Sundries, ...	3	1,755	85	Mar. 31	By Balance,..........		3,555 77
Mar. 3	To J. Bruce & Co	4	989	75				
" 15	To J. Dana & Co.....	5	1,039	92				
			6,128	14				6,128 14

Dr.				BILLS PAYABLE.				Cr.

1839					1839			
Feb. 15	To Cash,............	3	857	75	Jan. 9	By Merchandise,.....	1	857 75
Mar. 25	To do.	6	27	14	" 19	By C. Hammond,....	1	4,000 00
" 31	To Balance,..........		5,000	00	Feb. 25	By Merchandise,.....	3	1,000 00
					Mar. 1	By Insurance,........	4	27 14
			5,884	89				5,884 89

4

Dr.	CHARLES HAMMOND.	Cr.

1839					1839				
Jan. 19	To Bills Payable,....		4,000	00	Jan. 4	By Merchandise, ...	1	8,151	25
„ 29	To Cash,............	2	4,151	25	Feb. 1	By　　do.	2	583	40
Feb. 15	To Bills Receivable,.	3	785	50	„ 10	By　　do.	3	387	97
Mar. 31	To Balance,.........		185	87					
			9,122	62				9,122	62

Dr.	JAMES BRUCE & CO.	Cr.

1839					1839				
Jan. 6	To Merchandise,....	1	957	12	Jan. 25	By Bills Receivable, .	2	957	12
„ 30	To　　do.	2	989	75	Mar. 3	By　　do.	4	989	75
Feb. 28	To　　do.	4	1,579	23	„ 8	By Profit and Loss, ..	5	31	58
						By Balance,..........		1,547	65
			3,526	10				3,526	10

Dr.	JAMES PETERS.	Cr.

1839					1839				
Feb. 4	To Merchandise, ...	2	350	22	Feb. 8	By Bills Receivable, .	3	350	22
Mar. 5	To Smith's Sales,....	4	896	75	Mar. 31	By Balance, ...		896	75
			1,246	97				1,246	97

Dr.	RUFUS DEAN.	Cr.

1839					1839				
Feb. 4	To Merchandise, ...	2	575	88	Feb. 8	By Bills Receivable, .	3	575	88

Dr.	HENRY POPE.					Cr		
1839				1839				
Feb. 4	To Merchandise, ...	2	829	75	Feb. 8	By Bills Receivable, .		829	75

Dr.	BUCHANAN & CO.					Cr.		
1839				1839				
Mar. 7	To Cash,............	5	78	25	Feb. 10	By Merchandise,.....	3	78	25
" 21	To Smith's Sales,....	5	3,3·0	25	Mar. 31	By Balance,..........		3,3·0	25
			3,4··	50				3,438	5·

Dr.	JAMES FINLAY & CO.					Cr.		
1839				1839				
Mar. 25	To Cash,............	6	51	75	Feb. 10	By Merchandise, ...		51	75

Dr.	GEORGE SMITH.					Cr.		
1839				1839				
Mar. 1	To Sundries,........	4	93	48	Mar. 12	By Smith's Sales,....	5	775	58
" 19	To do.	4	2,759	88	" 25	By do.	6	3,045	09
" 31	To Balance, ...		9·7	31					
			3,·· 0	67				3,8·0	7

Dr.	J. DANA & CO.					Cr.		
1839				1839				
Mar. 1	To Sundries, ...	4	1,039	9·	Mar. 15	By Bills Receivable,.	5	1,039	92

11

6 Dr.	BALANCE.					Cr.	
1839	— Effects. —			1839	— Debts. —		
Mar. 31	To Cash,............	8,198	19	Mar. 31	By Bills Payable,....	5,000	00
	To Bills Receivable,.	3,555	77		By C. Hammond,....	185	87
	To Merchandise,.....	5,786	00		By George Smith,....	967	31
	To J. Bruce & Co....	1,547	65			6,153	18
	To James Peters,....	896	75		By Stock, net Capital,	17,191	36
	To Buchanan & Co..	3,360	25				
		23,344	54			23,344	54

EXPLANATION.

Cash. — The balance of this account, being the cash on hand, is part of your effects, and is therefore entered on the *Dr.* side of ' Balance.'

Bills Receivable. — The balance of this account, being the bills in hand, is also part of your effects, and is entered as before.

Bills Payable. — The balance of this account, being what *you* owe in accepted bills, is part of your debts, and is therefore entered on the *Cr.* side of ' Balance.'

Merchandise. — The balance of this account is the goods unsold, and is ascertained, in real business, by taking an Inventory. The difference between the two sides, *when the balance on hand is added to the sales,* is gain or loss, and is transferred to ' Profit and Loss.'

The *Personal* Accounts being debited for debts due to you, and credited for the reverse, the *differences* are consequently either your effects or debts, and are entered accordingly.

————

The ' Stock ' and ' Balance ' accounts are used merely on commencing or closing the books, no entry being made in them between one balance and another. They are, in fact, both statements of the merchant's Effects and Debts, and, if correct, must be alike. The ' Balance ' account is considered to be the converse of ' Stock ' account. It is composed of the *balances* of the several personal, money, and property accounts, and is therefore, simply an abstract of the Ledger.

ANALYSIS OF THE LEDGER.

Cash.
Receipts,................17,663 63
Payments,............... 9,465 51
Balance, in hand,........$8,198 12

Bills Receivable.
Received, ... 6,128 14
Disposed of, ... 2,572 37
Balance, in hand,........$3,555 77

Bills Payable.
Issued,.....~............ 5,884 89
Redeemed,.............. 884 89
Balance, outstanding,.....$5,000 00

Charles Hammond.
I owe him............... 9,122 62
He owes me............. 8,936 75
Balance, due him,........ $185 87

James Bruce & Co.
They owe me............ 3,526 10
I owe them.............. 1,978 45
Balance, in my favor,.....$1,547 65

James Peters
Owes me.................1,246 97
I owe him................ 350 22
Balance, in my favor,......$896 75

Buchanan & Co.
They owe me............3,438 50
I owe them.............. 78 25
Balance, in my favor, ...$3,360 25

George Smith
Owes me................3,820 67
I owe him................2,853 36
Balance, due him,... .....$977 31

Merchandise.
Total sales,..............11,073 90
Quantity unsold,..... .... 5,786 00
Returns, ...16,859 90
Deduct outlay,...........14,036 12
Gain,..................$2,823 78

For remarks on the method of adjusting property accounts, see page 70.

The above *balances* compose the entire property of the concern on the 31st March; and, when collected, the result is as follows : —

— Effects. —
Cash, ...in hand,......................8,198 12
Bills Receivable, ...   " 3,555 77
J. Bruce & Co...........owe me......................1,547 65
J. Peters................owes me...................... 896 75
Buchanan & Co..........owe me......................3,360 25
Merchandise,...........unsold, valued at.............5,786 00

Total amount of Effects,.........................23,344 54

— Deduct Debts, viz. —
Bills Payable,..........outstanding,..........5,000 00
C. Hammond,..........due him,.............. 185 87
George Smith,.........   "   .... 967 31 — 6,153 18

Net Capital, or present worth, ...$17,191 36

We next proceed to *prove* the accuracy of this statement by another process ; that is, by adding the net gain to the original capital, thus : —

— Gained —

By Merchandise, ... 2,823 78
By Commission, ... 264 87

Total *gains*, ... 3,088 65
Deduct, amount paid for charges, &c............. 897 29

Net gain,... 2,191 36
Add, capital commencing,....................... 15,000 00

Present worth, as before, ...:................. $17,191 36

Hence the merchant's net capital, or present worth, is ascertained by two distinct processes, the exact agreement of which constitutes a satisfactory and independent proof that his accounts are correctly stated and adjusted, namely : —

1. If from the total assets or effects you deduct his liabilities or debts, the difference* is his actual worth ; and,

2. If to the capital originally invested you add the gain, or deduct the loss, the result will be, as before, his present worth.

For the learner's convenience, we subjoin the 'Trial Balance,' and the 'Profit and Loss' and 'Balance' sheets, to the Introductory Set.

Drs.		TRIAL BALANCE. — *March* 31, 1839.	Crs.	
"	*"*	.....................................Stock,.....................................	15,000	00
35	13	..................................Profit and Loss,..........................		
1,235	00	......................................Charges,.................................	372	81
		....................................Commission,..............................	264	87
14,036	12	...................................Merchandise,.............................	11,073	90
17,663	63	....Cash,...................................	9,465	51
6,198	14	.................................Bills Receivable,..........................	2,572	37
884	89	..................................Bills Payable,............................	5,584	89
8,936	75	.................................Charles Hammond, ...	9,122	02
3,526	10	......................................J. Bruce & Co...........................	1,978	45
1,246	97	....................................James Peters,.............................	359	22
3,438	50	....................................Buchanan & Co...........................	78	25
2,853	3	.....................................George Smith,............................	3,830	67
59,934	59	......................................*Equilibrium*, ...	59,984	59

* This includes the original capital, increased by the gains, if the business has been profitable, but diminished by the losses, if the reverse.

Dr.	PROFIT AND LOSS SHEET.			Cr.	
To amount, posted,...........	35	13	By Merchandise,..............	2,823	78
To Charges,..................	8 2	16	By Commission, ...	2,4	87
To Stock, (net gain), ...	2, 91	3			
	3,088	65		3,0 8	65

Dr.	BALANCE SHEET.			Cr.	
To Cash, ...	8,198	12	By Bills Payable,..............	5,000	00
To Bills Receivable, ...	3,555	77	By C. Hammond,....	185	87
To Merchandise, ...4.........	5,78	00	By George Smith..............	9 7	31
To J. Bruce & Co..............	1,547	65	By Stock, (net capital,)........	17,191	3
To James Peters,..............	896	75			
To Buchanan & Co............	3,3 0	25			
	23,344	54		23,344	54

₊ The entries, in this set, arising at balancing, are not brought through the Journal, as recommended at page 72, but are simply transferred from one account in the Ledger to another.

ERRORS AND FRAUDS.

Absolute perfection in accounts has often been arrogated by writers upon this subject; but perfection never has been, and never can be, attained. However correct an art may be in theory, its practice is inevitably subject to errors; and no system, liable to intentional neglect or accidental perversion, is secure from the designs of the fraudulent or the consequences of carelessness.

The fundamental principles of Double Entry are as infallible in their application as their operation is extensive; but, in practice, they are exposed to all the moral and mental imperfections of the accountant; they are neither exempt from the defects of ignorance, the errors of indolence, nor the practices of fraud;

H

and frequent and careful investigation, on the part of the merchant himself, is scarcely sufficient to prevent such evils, where those who are intrusted with the management of his accounts are not entitled to implicit confidence.

The equality of debits and credits is the great systematic proof in book-keeping. This proof, however, is of a negative nature. *Without it*, the books cannot be correct ; *but with it*, they may be incorrect. It affords no check whatever on the first or primary entries, nor against those errors which are neutralized by counter entries so as not to affect the *equilibrium*. This neutralization of errors, being a remote chance, generally originates in design.

The principal cases in which errors can be committed, *without affecting the equality of debits and credits*, are,

1. One debit entry may be short-posted, and another over-posted the same amount.

2. One credit entry may be short-posted, and another over-posted the same amount.

3. A debit and credit entry may be equally short-posted.

4. A debit and credit entry may be equally over-posted.

5. Similar cases may occur in the *addition* of accounts.

6. Similar cases may occur in the *transfer* of accounts.

7. Similar cases may occur in the entry and carrying down of *balances*.

8. Another species of error consists in posting an amount correctly to the proper side, but to a *wrong* account. Thus $100, which properly belongs to a personal account, may be posted to a profit and loss or property account, without the cognizance of the systematic proof.

The common check against such fraudulent errors is that of calling over, comparing, and examining the books, by two persons, neither of whom posted the entries ; and all the *additions* and *transfers* must be revised and examined, as well as the general balance itself.

A book-keeper of practical experience, habitual accuracy, and tried integrity, is, however, of more value than all the checks that can be invented.

CHAPTER VII.

ON THE PRINCIPLES AND PRACTICE OF BOOK-KEEPING.

THE following queries and answers are intended to impress upon the mind the chief points in the art; and the learner will derive great advantage from an attentive study of them.

What is Book-keeping?

Book-keeping is the art of recording property, so as to show at all times the value of the whole capital and of each of its component parts.

By how many methods may books be kept?

The *form* and arrangement of books are varied according to the nature of the business; but there are, strictly speaking, only two methods of Book-keeping founded upon distinct principles, namely, *Single* and *Double* Entry.

What is meant by Single Entry?

SINGLE ENTRY chiefly records transactions by simply *debiting* the person who receives, and *crediting* the person who gives or delivers any thing. Of course the Ledger affords no other knowledge than the debts which are owing to the merchant and those he owes to others.

What is meant by Double Entry?

When each sum is entered *twice* in the Ledger, (hence Double Entry,) namely, on the *Dr.* side of one account, and on the *Cr.* side of some other account or accounts. The Ledger exhibits not only the debts due to, or by you, as in Single Entry, but also the cash and bills on hand, the amount of purchases and sales, and the gain or loss on each investment, or on the whole.

What is the use of the Day Book ?

The Day Book records every transaction which cannot be entered with propriety in the Subsidiary Books.

How many Subsidiary Books are generally used ?

This depends on the nature of the business; but the most usual are the following : — *Cash, Bill, Invoice, Book of Shipments,* and *Sales Book.*

What do the Subsidiary Books contain ?

The Cash Book contains all receipts and disbursements of money; the Bill Book, all bills received and accepted ; the Invoice Book, all goods purchased ; the Book of Shipments, all goods shipped off or exported ; and the Sales Book, the sales of all goods received on consignment.

What does the Account Current Book contain ?

It contains duplicates of the accounts of my correspondents as they stand in the Ledger, with the *particulars* of every item, arranged according to the dates, being an exact copy of the account transmitted or delivered to the party whose name it bears.

I. — THE LEDGER.

What is the design of the Ledger ?

The Ledger collects together articles of the same kind, under their respective heads. It is divided into several accounts, the *Dr.* and *Cr.* of which are opposite, to show how each account has been affected after these entries have been made.

What is meant by Dr. and Cr. ?

These terms are used, in a general sense, merely to distinguish the left from the right hand side of an account.

What do the accounts of Persons contain ?

On the *Dr.* side, the sums by which the person has become indebted to you ; and on the *Cr.* side, the sums by which you have become indebted to him.

What do accounts of Property contain ?

On the *Dr.* side, the cost, or value of what is on hand, at the beginning of the year, and what is afterwards purchased, with all charges connected with its cost; and on the *Cr.* side, the sales, and other returns.

What does the ' Cash ' account contain ?

On the *Dr.* side, the amount of money in hand, when tne books are opened, and all sums subsequently *received;* and on the *Cr.* side, all disbursements, or moneys *paid* out.

What does the account of ' Bills Receivable' contain?

On the *Dr.* side, the amount of all bills *received;* and on the *Cr.* side, the amount of all such bills as are *paid,* or otherwise disposed of.

What does the account of ' Bills Payable' contain?

On the *Cr.* side, the amount of all bills or acceptances *issued* by the concern; and on the *Cr.* side, the amount of all such bills as are *paid* or withdrawn from circulation.

What does the ' Stock' account contain?

On the *Dr.* side, the debts or liabilities of the concern commencing, and on the *Cr.* side, the total sum of the assets or effects ; — in other words, this account contains a statement of the whole capital, collectively, without designating its constituent parts.

What does the ' Profit and Loss' account contain?

On the *Dr.* side, all losses incurred in the business ; and on the *Cr.* side, all the gains made.

II. — JOURNALIZING.

What is the use of the Journal?

The Journal contains an arrangement of the transactions, collected monthly from the Subsidiary Books, with the *Drs.* and *Crs.* pointed out, in order that they may be easily posted to the Ledger.

What is the GENERAL *rule for Journalizing?*

The thing *received,* or person accountable to me, is *Dr.,* and the thing *delivered,* or person to whom I am accountable, is *Cr.*

Explain this rule more particularly.

The accounts of *persons* are *debited* when individuals become indebted to me, and *credited* when I become indebted to them.

The accounts of money are *debited* for all sums *received,* and credited for all sums *paid.*

The accounts of property are *debited* for its cost, or value, and credited for the sales, or returns.

' Profit and Loss,' or its subsidiary accounts, is *debited* for every loss, or charge against the business, and *credited* for the gains.

12   H *

How is the CASH BOOK *Journalized monthly?*

For all moneys received, ... CASH *Dr. to Sundries;*

For all moneys paid, ... SUNDRIES *Dr. to Cash;*
specifying particulars, and classing items of the same kind together.

What is the rule for making ' CASH *' Dr. in some cases, and Cr. in others?*

The rule is simple and uniform. For all moneys *received* cash is Dr., and for all moneys *paid* Cash is Cr.

How is the BILL BOOK *Journalized monthly?*

For all bills received, . . BILLS RECEIVABLE *Dr. to Sundries;*

For all bills accepted, . . SUNDRIES *Dr. to Bills Payable;*
specifying particulars and combining the items belonging to similar accounts so that the totals may be posted in one sum to the Ledger.

How are the purchases of goods Journalized?

MERCHANDISE *Dr. to Sundries,* viz.

To A. B. C., &c., (the sellers,) each, for the amount of his invoice, during the month.

How are the sales of goods Journalized?

SUNDRIES *Dr. to Merchandise,* viz.

A. B. C., &c., (the purchasers,) each for the amount of his purchases during the month.

How are the following transactions Journalized?

1. *When you ship goods abroad in consequence of orders?*

A. B. (on whose account) *Dr. to Sundries,* viz.

    To Merchandise, ... for amount of goods.

    To Charges, ... for charges at shipping.

    To Commission, ... for my commission.

    To Insurance, ... for premium and policy.

2. *When you ship goods abroad as an adventure?*

ADVENTURE TO —— *Dr. to Sundries,* viz.

    To Merchandise, ... for the amount.

' *To Charges,* . . . . for charges at shipping.

    To Insurance, ... for premium and policy.

When the Agent renders you an Account Sales?

A. B. (the agent) *Dr. to Adventure to* —— for the net proceeds, which if greater than the outset charge, the difference is gain.

How is the account closed ?

ADVENTURE TO —— *Dr. to Profit and Loss ;* but if there has been a loss, this entry is reversed.

When you sell goods on Commission, how are such transactions Journalized ?

Enter ... The PURCHASER *Dr. to Sales of Consignments,* specifying the article, terms, and amount.

When the Sales are closed, what is the Journal entry ?

SALES OF CONSIGNMENTS *Dr. to Sundries.*

> *To Insurance,* . . . . for premium and policy.
> *To Charges,* . . . . for duty, freight, &c.
> *To Commission,* . . . . on insurance and sales.
> *To A. B. (the consigner,)* . . . for net proceeds.

How are the following transactions in BANKRUPTCY stated ?

1. *When the failure is a total loss ?*

PROFIT AND LOSS *Dr. to A. B., (the Bankrupt,)* for the amount of my claim.

2. *When a partial loss is sustained ?*

PROFIT AND LOSS *Dr. to A. B.,* for the sum lost by his failure.

III. — POSTING AND COMPARING THE BOOKS.

What is meant by Posting ?

Posting is the process of transferring the Journal entries into the Ledger.

What is the GENERAL rule for posting ?

Debit the account that is *Dr.* ' *To* ' the *title* of that which is *Cr.*, and credit the account that is *Cr.* ' *By* ' the *title* of that which is *Dr.*

When an entry is posted, what do you do next ?

Place in the marginal column of the JOURNAL the folio of the *Ledger* where the entry is made, and in the LEDGER the page of the *Journal* from which it is transferred.

What is meant by COMPARING the books ?

Examining every entry before it is posted ; because a mistake in any of the Subsidiary Books must necessarily run through the Journal and Ledger.

How is this accomplished ?

After Journalizing the Subsidiary Books, the Journal must be carefully compared with each book before posting.

What is the best plan of comparing the Journal and Ledger?

By two persons.   One has the Journal, and reads the *Ledger* folio, the title of the account, and the *Drs.* and *Crs.*; while the other turns to the Ledger, and marks off the entry with a dot, (or ✓) if correct.   The dots in the Journal show how far the comparison is advanced, and the marks in the Ledger show what entries are compared.

How is it known when the comparison is finished?

By glancing over the Ledger, and finding the mark of comparison affixed to each item.   If the mark is not so affixed, turn to the entry in the Journal which had not been marked, and observe if it be right.

What is the best plan to rectify omissions?

By inserting the article omitted under the last entry, when you discover the omission, and making a cross thus + against it on the margin, and another at the place where it should have been.

If you have written a line entirely wrong, or in a wrong place, how do you proceed?

Write the word *error* at the end, prefix a cross, and omit or cancel the sum.

How should errors be cancelled?

By drawing a line lightly through them, so that the old writing may still be legible; by which it will be evident the book has not been vitiated for a fraudulent purpose; and the same method should be followed in correcting errors in the Journal.

IV.— BALANCING THE LEDGER.

What is meant by BALANCING?

It is the equilibrating of, or making equal, all the accounts.

What is the design of balancing the Ledger?

To collect the various branches of business into a concise abstract, so as to show the debts owing to and by you, the property on hand, together with the gain you have made, or the loss sustained, since you began business, or since a former balance.

What is meant by the Balance of an account ?

The difference between the *Dr.* and *Cr.* sides, if the account be properly adjusted, which must constitute a part of my effects or debts.

How are accounts of Persons balanced ?

First. If the *Dr.* side be greater, credit the account ' *By Balance* ' for the difference ; being a debt owing *to* me.

Second. If the *Cr.* side be greater, debit it ' *To Balance* ' for the difference ; being a debt due *by* me ; carrying down the *balance* on the opposite side of the account, which is done in the same manner with every one that has a balance, whether accounts of persons or property.

How is the 'Cash' account balanced ?

Credit it ' *By Balance* ' for the *difference* ; being the cash in hand.

How is the account of 'Bills Receivable' balanced ?

Credit it ' *By Balance* ' for the *difference ;* being the bills on hand in my favor.

How is the account of ' Bills Payable ' balanced ?

Debit it ' *To Balance* ' for the *difference ;* being the bills or acceptances unpaid, or outstanding.

How are Property accounts, such as Merchandise, Ships, Houses, Lands, and the like, balanced when the whole is unsold?

' *By Balance*,' for its cost or present value.

How are such accounts balanced when only a part is sold?

Credit each respective account ' *By Balance*,' for the value of the property unsold : the difference between the two sides will then exhibit the gain or loss on the quantity sold, which difference must be transferred to the proper side of the ' Profit and Loss ' account.

How are the accounts of Merchandise, &c., balanced when the whole is sold?

If the *Cr.* side be greater, the *difference* is *gain*, which is closed by entering on the *Dr.* side, ' *To Profit and Loss*.' If the *Dr.* side be greater, the difference is *loss*, and is therefore entered on the *Cr.* side, ' *By Profit and Loss ;* ' transferring the sum to the proper side of ' Profit and Loss.'

How are Shipments or Adventures balanced ?

In the same manner as the account of ' Merchandise.'

How are the accounts of 'Charges,' 'Interest,' and 'Commission' closed?

' *To* ' or ' *By Profit and Loss*,' as the case may require.

How is ' Profit and Loss ' account closed?

By transferring the result, if *gain*, to the *Cr.* side ; but if *loss*, to the *Dr.* side, of 'Stock.'

How is the ' Stock ' account closed?

' *To Balance* ' for net capital, or '*By Balance*' for net deficiency.

V. — GENERAL BALANCE.

How is a statement of your affairs made out?

By collecting all the balances of the accounts, being my effects and debts, and arranging them in the form of *Dr.* and *Cr.*

Explain particularly how the 'Balance' account is to be arranged.

A sheet of paper is ruled in the form of *Dr.* and *Cr.*, with money columns, and headed as follows :

Dr.	Balance.	Cr.
On the *Dr.* side place the assets, or balances in your favor; and		On the *Cr.* side place the debts, or liabilities of the concern.

$*_{*}*$ The difference exhibits your net capital, if the *Dr.* side be greater ; but if the *Cr.* exceed the *Dr.*, the concern is insolvent, and the difference shows the deficiency.

Why ought the difference of the ' Stock ' account to agree with that of ' Balance '?

The ' Stock' account shows the net Capital, abstractly considered, and the other balances show its component parts. If, therefore, an extract be made of the latter, their sum must be equal to the balance of ' Stock ; ' in which equality consists the great proof that the accounts are properly adjusted.

VI. — MERCHANTS' ACCOUNTS.

What is an Account Sales ?

It is an account of goods sold on *commission*, drawn out by the agent, and sent to his employer, who made the consignment.

What is meant by the Net Proceeds ?

The sum that remains after all charges attending the sales have been deducted, which sum is due to the person from whom you received the consignment.

What is meant by an Account Current ?

An Account Current is a statement of our mercantile transactions with any person, drawn out in a plain, circumstantial manner, arranged in the form of *Dr.* and *Cr.*

Does it require a knowledge of Book-keeping to understand the nature of an Account Current ?

Yes ; because the transactions are narrated as expressed in the Journal; and where the collective term *Sundries* occurs in the Ledger, every particular is supplied.

VII. — PARTNERSHIP ACCOUNTS.

What is Partnership ?

Partnership is a contract entered into by two or more persons to carry on a certain trade or business, for which they agree to join either their money, labor, or skill, or all of them, and to divide the gain or sustain the loss agreeably to the terms of copartnership.

How should the books of a copartnership be kept ?

As if they belonged to one person only ; but the plural number should be used — *we, us,* and *ours,* instead of *I, me, mine,* and the like.

When the capital to be employed in the concern is fixed upon, how should it be entered ?

SUNDRIES *Dr. to Stock ;* each partner for his share or proportion.

When these shares are paid in?

CASH, or the article, *Dr. to Sundries;* to each partner for the amount of his share.

Is one account, in general, sufficient for each partner?

Yes ; and it should be kept in the same manner as that of any neutral person.

What should the partners' accounts exhibit?

They should exhibit only the money paid, or any other articles taken from the concern for private use, together with the interest on their respective shares.

How are the partners' accounts closed?

The balance is carried forward, like any other personal account, until the profits are divided, or an alteration in the shares takes place, or the term of the copartnership expires ; previous to which these accounts must be closed.

When the profits are to be divided among the partners?

Enter PROFIT AND LOSS *Dr. to each partner,* for his individual share.

When the profits are to be applied to increase the stock?

PROFIT AND LOSS *Dr. to Stock.*

If there has been a loss on the business?

The above entries are reversed.

When an alteration in the shares takes place?

The books must be previously balanced, and the partners' accounts closed.

What is the Stock to be considered?

As a joint account, to be divided at such periods and in such proportions as are directed by the articles of copartnership.

What should the ' Stock' account exhibit?

The amount or value of the company's effects, both real and personal.

SET I.

WHOLESALE DEALER'S BOOKS.

CONCERN, ... INDIVIDUAL.
CAPITAL, ... VARIABLE.
BUSINESS, ... COMMENCED.
RESULT, ... PROFITABLE.

OBSERVATIONS.

To avoid increasing the number of the Subsidiary Books, every transaction, except the money received and paid, is entered in the Day Book. The Journal, therefore, is, in the present set, composed from the Cash Book and Day Book, and contains a *monthly* abstract of the respective transactions. The concern is supposed to commence on the first of January, 1839, with a cash capital of $10,000; and hence there is no inventory of Effects and Debts at this date. The books are opened by simply debiting Cash to Stock for the money in hand, which constitutes the capital invested in the business.

It is a common opinion, that, from the nature of his business, the retailer is unable to keep his books by Double Entry, or in the same systematic manner as those of the wholesale dealer or merchant. The difficulty, however, applies solely to the quantities of goods, and in no respect to the accounts, which are, in all kinds of business, composed of expenditure and returns, receipts

13   I

and payments. These particulars the retailer can record as easily as the merchant; and therefore he may, with equal facility, systematize his accounts.

The following directions will enable the learner to arrange the Journal entries in a correct and proper manner.

1. The *Cash Book*, pages 102 and 103, and the *Day Book*, pages 107 to 112, should be transcribed into a book prepared for the purpose.

In the Ledger, the *Cash account* is debited for all moneys received, and credited for all moneys paid. Therefore, to Journalize the cash items, say,

Cash Dr. to Sundries, viz.

To the respective accounts on the left-hand side of the Cash Book, for the sums received; and

Sundries Dr. to Cash, viz.

The several accounts on the right-hand side, for the sums paid; specifying dates, and classing similar entries together.

When cash has been received upon only *one* account, 'Cash' is made *Dr.* to that account; and when cash has been paid upon only *one* account, that account is made *Dr.* to 'Cash.' When cash has been received or paid more than once upon the same account during the month, the different receipts or payments are to be collected in the inner column, and the total sum only is to be carried to account.

As soon as each sum is entered in the Journal, mark it off on the dollar column in the Cash Book, thus √, which will readily direct the eye to those entries which still remain, and prevent omissions.

2. Having Journalized the cash transactions for the month of January, agreeably to the above directions, turn to the *Day Book*, and arrange the purchases, sales, &c., in a similar manner. For example, the account of *'Merchandise'* is debited for all goods purchased, and credited for the sales or other returns. Therefore, to Journalize the Day Book, say,

MERCHANDISE *Dr. to* SUNDRIES.
For the purchases, viz.

To each seller for the amount bought of him during the month ; and

SUNDRIES *Dr. to* MERCHANDISE,
For the sales, viz.

Each purchaser for the amount sold him.

If several sales are made to the same individual, at different dates during the month, collect the amounts in the inner column, and extend the total only in the debit column.

3. The account of 'Bills Receivable' is debited for all bills *received*, and the account of 'Bills Payable' is credited for all bills *issued* or *accepted*. Therefore, to Journalize the bill transactions, say,

BILLS RECEIVABLE *Dr. to* SUNDRIES,
For the bills received, viz.

To the several individuals on whose account bills were received during the month ; and

SUNDRIES *Dr. to* BILLS PAYABLE,
For the bills issued, viz.

The several persons on whose account the bills were issued ; specifying dates, and observing to collect in the inner money column, all the bills received or issued on the same account during the month.

To facilitate this process of Journalizing, the respective items belonging to each account should be arranged, for reference, by means of the dates. Take, for illustration, the transactions for January, Day Book, page 106. Fold a sheet of paper in two parts, and arrange the purchases and sales under the proper titles, as follows : —

JANUARY, 1839.

Merchandise Dr. to Sundries.	*Sundries Dr. to Merchandise.*
To J. Andrews & Co. 1st, 21st.	Thomas Harris, 9th, 14th, 18th.
To W. Smith, ... 4th, 23d.	B. Canfield, . . 10th, 15th, 22d.
To Bird and Beardsley, 8th, 15th.	Edward Ford, 1th, 16th, 23d, 31st.
To Bills Payable, . . . 30th.	C. Drummond, 28th.
	Bills Receivable, 29th.

An index similar to the preceding must be made at the end of each month, which will enable the book-keeper to classify and combine entries under their appropriate titles with ease and facility. The index being completed, turn, by the help of the *date*, to the transaction, and, in every case where several purchases, sales, &c., have been made from or by the same person, during the month, enter the amounts of each in the inner column, and carry the total only to the Ledger.

In the arrangement of the *Journal*, the Debit and Credit posting amounts are entered in distinct money columns, the advantage of which is that both columns can be added up separately ; and as they contain the same amounts, although consisting of different items, they form a most certain check on the additions of each page, and insure correct periodical totals. This will be found of the greatest utility in proving the postings to the Ledger. See illustration, page 124.

CASH BOOK.—Set I

Dr.	CASH.			
1839				
Jan. 1	To Stock,...........for capital in trade,......		10,000	00
" 14	To Thomas Harris,....received from him,......		280	00
" 25	To Edward Ford,...... " " "		150	00
" 28	To Benjamin Canfield,. " " "		100	00
" 31	To Merchandise,......for cash sales, ⅌ C. S. B...		1,470	00
			12,000	00
	. *Ent⁴ Journal, fol.* 1.			
	Balance, from January, ...		8,100	00
Feb. 1	To Bills Receivable,...No. 1, discounted, ⅌ B. B..		1,350	00
" 2	To J. Thompson & Son, rec⁴ from them,........		108	00
" 5	To Merchandise,......for cash sales, ⅌ C. S. B..		1,250	00
" 10	To J. Thompson & Son, for draft on Hill, ...		500	00
" "	To Bills Receivable,...No. 2, discounted, ⅌ B. B.		3,470	00
" 28	To Merchandise,......for cash sales, ⅌ C. S. B		522	00
			15,300	00
	Ent⁴ Journal, fol. 2.			
	Balance, from February,..		8,730	00
Mar. 4	To Bills Receivable,...No. 6, discounted, ⅌ B.B..		1,895	00
" 6	To Thomas Harris,....received from him,......		150	00
" 12	To Merchandise,......for cash sales, ⅌ C. S. B..		176	00
" 18	To Benjamin Canfield,.received from him,......		75	00
" 20	To Bills Receivable,...No. 7,...........$2,875			
" 22	" " " No. 3,...... 322			
" "	" " " No. 4,........... 1,322		4,519	00
" 30	To Merchandise,......for cash sales, ⅌ C. S. B..		260	00
			15,805	00
	Ent⁴ Journal, fol. 3.			

	CONTRA.		Cr.	
1839				
Jan. 3	By Merchandise,......for goods bought at auction,		1,750	00
" 10	By Charges,..........paid for store fixtures,&c.		150	00
" 14	By J. Andrews & Co... " them, ℔ receipt,.....		1,500	00
" 28	By William Smith,.... " him, ℔ do.		500	00
	Balance, to February,....		8,100	00
			12,000	00
	Ent<u>d</u> Journal, fol. 1.			
Feb. 1	By Profit and Loss,....paid discount on bill No. 1,		6	75
" 10	By Merchandise,...... " freight,&c. ℔ Ontario,		58	25
" "	By Profit and Loss,.... " discount on bill No. 2,		52	00
" 15	By Charges,.......... " ℔ Petty Cash Book,..		75	00
" 20	By Merchandise,...... " for Cassimeres,......		1,578	00
" 28	By J. Brown & Co.....remitted to the.a,........		4,800	00
	Balance, to March,.......		8,730	00
			15,300	00
	Ent<u>d</u> Journal, fol. 2.			
Mar. 4	By Profit and Loss,....paid discount on bill No. 6,		18	95
" "	By Bills Payable,..... " No. 1, due this day,..		3,870	00
" 8	By J. Andrews & Co... " them, ℔ receipt,.....		500	00
" 9	By Bills Payable,..... " No. 4, due this day,..		1,025	00
" 15	By Charges,.......... " ℔ Petty Cash Book,..		115	05
" 19	By Merchandise,......for goods purch'd this day,		5,397	00
" 25	By J. Andrews & Co...paid their draft, at sight,..		1,075	00
" 30	By Charges,.......... " clerks' salaries, &c...		350	00
	Balance, on hand,.......		3,454	00
			15,805	00
	Ent<u>d</u> Journal, fol. 3.			

REMARKS ON THE CASH BOOK.

The most important purposes for which this book is kept are, to enable the cashier, or person who has charge of the cash department, to ascertain, at any time, the money he has *received* and *paid*, and also how much he ought still to have in hand. The keeping of it correctly, therefore, is an object of the greatest consequence.

In extensive establishments, it is found necessary to keep a *Petty Cash Book* for entering small items of expense, which would be inconvenient to bring, separately, through the principal Cash Book. The amount of such petty expenditures is generally entered at stated periods (for instance, once a month) in the Cash Book.

When money is borrowed or lent for a few days, which frequently happens in business, it is unnecessary to carry such sums into the Journal and Ledger: it is sufficient to short extend such entries in the Cash Book, and, when paid, they, of course, balance themselves.

When one page of the Cash Book becomes full before the end of the month, both pages must be added, the amounts placed opposite to each other, the blank page filled up with a diagonal line, and the amounts of both pages carried forward. The same method, when necessary, is adopted at the end of the month.

The reason for Journalizing cash transactions first is, that the Cash Book is always balanced the last day of the month, and after that period can receive no additional entries ; but the Day Book may be left open, and one or more blank pages be reserved for closing accounts, and other occurrences, which will be in time to be Journalized in their proper place during the month.

DAY BOOK.—Set 1

1	NEW YORK, *January* 1, 1839.		
1	Bought of James Andrews & Co. Merchandise, amounting, ℣ Invoice, to..........	3,500	00
	——— 4 ———		
1	Bought of William Smith, Merchandise, amounting, ℣ Invoice, to..........	1,500	00
	——— 8 ———		
1	Bought of Bird & Beardsley, 15 pieces Cassimeres, amounting to.............	850	00
	——— 9 ———		
1	Sold Thomas Harris, 2 pieces Blue Cloth, 56 yds.....@ 40/..........	280	00
	——— 10 ———		
1	Sold Benjamin Canfield, 1 piece Cassimere, 29 yds......@ 20/..........	72	50
	——— 12 ———		
1	Sold Edward Ford, 3 pieces Cassimere, 80 yds.....@ 20/..........	200	00
	——— 14 ———		
1	Sold Thomas Harris, 8 pieces Cassimere, 200 yds....@ 16/..........	400	00
	——— 15 ———		
1	Sold Benjamin Canfield, 2 pieces Cassimere, 56 yds.....@ 20/..........	140	00
	——— " ———		
1	Bought of Bird & Beardsley, 1 bale Sheetings, amounting to................	175	00
	——— 16 ———		
1	Sold Edward Ford, 1 piece Cassimere, 28 yds.....@ 20/.... 70 00 1 " Blue Cloth, 24 " .....@ 40/....120 00	190	00
	——— 18 ———		
1	Sold Thomas Harris, 10 pieces Black Cloth, 250 yds..@ 64/...2,000 00 10 " Blue do. 240 " ..@ 40/...1,200 00	3,200	00

		2
NEW YORK, *January* 21, 1839.		

1	Bought of James Andrews & Co. Merchandise, amounting, ℙ Invoice, to..........	2,500	00
	———— 22 ————		
1	Sold Benjamin Canfield, 60 pieces Cotton Sheetings,....@ 28/..........	210	00
	———— 23 ————		
1	Sold Edward Ford, 1 piece Black Cloth, 28 yds.....@ 56/....196 00 1 ″ Blue do. 25 ″ ....@ 40/....125 00 1 ″ Brown do. 21 ″ ....@ 24/.... 63 00 1 ″ Cassimere,..26 ″ ....@ 20/.... 65 00 Box, &c.................. 1 00	450	00
	———— ″ ————		
1	Bought of William Smith, Merchandise, ℙ Invoice,.....................	560	00
	———— 28 ————		
1	Sold Charles Drummond, 3 pieces Black Cloth, 84 yds...@ 48/....504 00 4 ″ Blue do. 110 ″ ...@ 40/....550 00 8 ″ Brown do. 210 ″ ...@ 32/....840 00 Box and cartage,.......... 1 00	1,895	00
	———— 29 ————		
1	Sold J. Robinson, Merchandise, ℙ B. P., for which I have received his Promissory Note, at 90 days' date, No. 1, due May 2,...............................	1,350	00
	———— 30 ————		
1	Bought at auction this day, 3 bales of Broadcloth, ℙ Invoice, amounting to $3,870, for which I gave in settlement my Acceptance, at 30 days' date, No. 1, due 4 Mar.,	3,870	00
	———— 31 ————		
1	Sold Edward Ford, 2 pieces Black Cloth, 53 yds....@ 32/....212 00 2 ″ Blue do. 84 ″ ....@ 40/....420 00	632	00

3	NEW YORK, *February* 1, 1839.		
2	Sold J. Thompson & Son, 2 pieces Cassimere, 54 yds.....@ 16/..........		108	00
	——— 2 ———			
2	Sold Benjamin Canfield, 3 pieces Black Cloth, 84 yds....@ 40/....420 00 4 " Cassimere, 70 " ....@ 20/....175 00		595	00
	——— 5 ———			
2	Accepted a Bill drawn by J. Andrews & Co., at 30 days' date, No. 2, due March 10,..............		2,000	00
	——— 7 ———			
2	Sold J. Thompson & Son, 3 pieces Blue Cloth, 81 yds....@ 48/..........		486	00
	——— 9 ———			
2	Received from Thomas Harris his Promissory Note, at 90 days' date, No. 2, due May 13,..............		3,470	00
	——— " ———			
2	Allowed Thomas Harris, on settlement this day, an abatement of...............................		130	00
	——— 13 ———			
2	Received ℔ ship Ontario, from London, 10 bales Broadcloth, shipped by Jas. Brown & Co., pursuant to order, and for my account and risk, amounting, ℔ Invoice, to £1,000: Exchange, $4 80 ℔ £...............................		4,800	00
	——— 14 ———			
2	Passed Bonds at Custom-House for Duties on the above Goods, at 6 and 9 months,....................		2,400	00
	——— " ———			
2	Accepted a Draft drawn by William Smith in favor of T. Jones, at 60 days' date, No. 3, due April 18,...		1,000	00
	——— 15 ———			
2	Sold Benjamin Canfield, 10 pieces Blue Cloth, 280 yds...@ 40/..1,400 00 5 " Black do. 150 " ...@ 32/.. 600 00		2,000	00

	NEW YORK, *February* 17, 1839.		**4**
2	Received from Benjamin Canfield his Acceptance, at 30 days' date, in full for Account rendered, No. 3, due March 22,..............	322	50
	———————— 18 ————————		
2	Sold John Thompson & Son, 5 p! Black Cloth, 140 yds.......@ 32/....560 00 3 " Blue do. 81 " ....@ 24/....243 00 4 " Mix'd Cassimere, 110 yds...@ 20/....275 00 Box and cartage,............ 1 50	1,079	50
	———————— 19 ————————		
2	Received from Edward Ford his Note of Hand, payable 1 month from date, No. 4, due 22d March,.......	1,322	00
	———————— 24 ————————		
2	Accepted Bird & Beardsley's Draft in favor of H. Smith, payable 10 days from date, No. 4, due 9 March,....................................	1,025	00
	———————— 26 ————————		
2	Sold at auction a quantity of Merchandise, for which I have received Brown & S n's Promissory Note, at 6 months' date, No. 5, due 29 August,.........	3,506	00
	———————— 27 ————————		
2	Sold Benjamin Canfield, 1 piece Brown Mix'd Cloth, 28 yds. @ 48/.168 00 1 " Drab " " 28 " @ 32/.112 00	280	00
	———————— 28 ————————		
2	Sold Edward Ford, 2 pieces Black Cloth, 55 yds....@ 40/..........	275	00
	———————— " ————————		
2	Accepted a Bill drawn by J. Andrews & Co. in favor of themselves, at 30 days' date, No. 5, due 2 April,	2,500	00

5	**NEW YORK,** *March* 1, 1839.		
3	Bought of Bird & Beardsley, Merchandise, ℣ B. P., amounting to............	1756	00
	——————— 2 ———————		
3	Sold Thomas Harris, 1 piece Broadcloth, 26 yds......@ 40/....130 00 1 " Cassimere, 28 " .....@ 20/.... 70 00 1 " Sheeting, 28 " .....@ 1/6... 5 25	205	25
	——————— 4 ———————		
3	Received from Charles Drummond his Promissory Note, at 60 days' date, No. 6, due 6th May, ...	1,895	00
	——————— 5 ———————		
3	Sold Thomas Harris, 2 pieces Cotton Sheeting, 56 yds. @ 1/6... 10 50 3 " Blk. Broadcloth, 84 " @ 32/....336 00 2 " Blue Cassimere, 55¼ " @ 16/....110 50	457	00
	——————— 6 ———————		
3	Bought of Bird & Beardsley, Merchandise, ℣ B. P., amounting to	500	00
	——————— 7 ———————		
3	Received of B. Canfield a Draft on Brown, Brothers, & Co., at 10 days' sight, No. 7, due 20th March, ..	2,875	00
	——————— 8 ———————		
3	Bought of James Andrews & Co. Merchandise, amounting, ℣ B. P., to............	1,575	00
	——————— " ———————		
3	Sold Benjamin Canfield, 3 pieces Blue Cloth, 84 yds...@ 48/....504 00 2 " Black do. 35 " ...@ 40/....175 00 10 " Cotton Sheeting,......@ 40/.... 50 00	729	00
	——————— 9 ———————		
3	Sold Walter Jones, A quantity of Merchandise, for which I have re- ceived in payment *my* Acceptance in favor of J. Andrews & Co., due 10th inst., No. 2,........	2,000	00

	NEW YORK, *March* 12, 1839.			6
3	Bought of William Smith, 1 bale Cotton Sheeting, ℔ B. P.................		375	00
	———— 15 ————			
3	Sold Benjamin Canfield, 10 pieces Cotton Sheeting,.....@ 40/.... 50 00 2 " Blk. Cassimere, 54 yds.@ 16/....108 00 3 dozen Cotton Hose,........@ 24/.... 9 00		167	00
	———— 18 ————			
3	Bought of J. Andrews & Co. 11 pieces Mix'd Cloth, 154 yds..@ 24/........		462	00
	———— 20 ————			
3	Sold Charles Drummond, 4 pieces Cotton Sheeting,......@ 40/.... 20 00 3 " Mix'd Cloth, .-.42 yds.@ 32/....168 00 4 " Blue Cassimere, 110 " @ 16/....220 00		408	00
	———— 25 ————			
3	Sold J. Thompson & Son, 2 pieces Black Cloth, 56 yds....@ 24/....168 00 4 " Blue do. 118 " ....@ 32/....472 00		640	00
	———— 26 ————			
3	Sold Edward Ford, 3 pieces Blk. Cassimere, 84 yds. @ 24/..........		252	00
	———— 28 ————			
3	Sold Thomas Harris, 1 piece Blue Cloth, 27 yds......@ 32/....108 00 1 " Cassimere, 28 " ......@ 16/.... 56 00		164	00
	———— 29 ————			
3	Sold Charles Drummond, 3 pieces Cassimere, 81 yds.....@ 16/..........		162	00
	———— 30 ————			
3	Sold J. Thompson & Son, 4 pieces Blue Cloth, 112 yds....@ 48/..........		672	00

JOURNAL. — SET I.

1							
		JANUARY, 1839.					

			— Drs. —		— Crs. —	
1	CASH *Dr. to* SUNDRIES,.................	12,000	00			
1	To Stock, ... 1st,..............		......	..	10,000	00
3	To Thomas Harris, ...14th,..............		......	..	280	00
4	To Edward Ford, ...25th,..............		......	..	150	00
3	To Benjamin Canfield,.....28th,..............		......	..	100	00
1	To Merchandise, ...31st,..............		......	..	1,470	00
1	SUNDRIES *Dr. to* CASH,..................		......	..	3,900	00
1	Merchandise, ... 3d,..............	1,750	00			
1	Charges, ...10th,..............	150	00			
2	J. Andrews & Co.........14th,..............	1,500	00			
3	William Smith, ...28th,..............	500	00			
1	MERCHANDISE *Dr. to* SUNDRIES,.........	12,955	00			
2	To J. Andrews & Co....... 1st,......3,500 00 21st,......2,500 00		......	..	6,000	00
3	To William Smith,........ 4th,......1,500 00 23d,...... 560 00		......	..	2,060	00
3	To Bird & Beardsley,..... 8th, ... 850 00 15th, ... 175 00		......	..	1,025	00
2	To Bills Payable,.........30th,..............		......	..	3,870	00
1	SUNDRIES *Dr. to* MERCHANDISE,.........		......	..	9,019	50
3	Thomas Harris, ... 9th, ... 280 00 14th, ... 400 00 18th, ...3,200 00	3,880	00			
3	Benjamin Canfield,........10th, ... 72 50 15th, ... 140 00 22d, ... 210 00	422	50			
4	Edward Ford,............12th, ... 200 00 16th, ... 190 00 23d, ... 450 00 31st, ... 632 00	1,472	00			
4	Charles Drummond,.......28th,..............	1,895	00			
2	Bills Receivable, ...29th,..............	1,350	00			
			37,874	50	37,874	50

FEBRUARY, 1839. 2

		— Drs. —	— Crs. —
2	CASH *Dr. to* SUNDRIES,.................	7,200 00	
2	To Bills Receivable, ... 1st, ...1,350 00		
	13th,.......3,470 00	....	4,820 00
4	To J. Thompson & Son,... 2d,...... 108 00		
	10th,....... 500 00	....	608 00
1	To Merchandise, ... 5th,.......1,250 00		
	28th,....... 522 00	....	1,772 00
2	SUNDRIES *Dr. to* CASH,.................	....	6,570 00
1	Profit and Loss,........... 1st,....... 6 75		
	15th,....... 52 00	58 75	
1	Merchandise, ...13th,....... 58 25		
	20th,.......1,578 00	1,636 25	
1	Charges,.................17th,.............	75 00	
4	J. Brown & Co...........28th,.............	4,800 00	
1	MERCHANDISE *Dr. to* SUNDRIES,.........	7,200 00	
4	To J. Brown & Co........13th,.............	....	4,800 00
2	To Bills Payable,.........14th,.............	....	2,400 00
1	SUNDRIES *Dr. to* MERCHANDISE,.........	....	8,329 50
4	J. Thompson & Son,....... 1st,....... 108 00		
	7th,....... 486 00		
	18th,.......1,079 50	1,673 50	
3	Benjamin Canfield,........ 2d, ... 595 00		
	15th,.......2,000 00		
	27th,....... 280 00	2,875 00	
2	Bills Receivable,..........26th,.............	3,506 00	
4	Edward Ford,............28th,.............	275 00	
2	SUNDRIES *Dr. to* BILLS PAYABLE,........	....	6,525 00
2	J. Andrews & Co......... 5th,.......2,000 00		
	28th,.......2,500 00	4,500 00	
3	William Smith,...........14th,.............	1,000 00	
3	Bird & Beardsley,........24th,.............	1,025 00	
2	BILLS RECEIVABLE *Dr. to* SUNDRIES,....	5,114 50	
3	To Thomas Harris, ... 9th,.............	....	3,470 00
3	To Benjamin Canfield, ...17th,.............	....	322 50
4	To Edward Ford,. ....19th,.............	....	1,322 00
1	PROFIT AND LOSS *Dr. to* T. HARRIS,		
3	*For abatement allowed him,* 12th,..............	130 00	130 00
		41,069 00	41,069 00

	3 MARCH, 1839.		— Drs. —		— Crs. —	
2	CASH *Dr. to* SUNDRIES,...............		7,075	00		
2	To Bills Receivable,...... 4th,.......1,895 00					
	22d,.......4,519 00		......	..	6,414	00
3	To Thomas Harris, ...12th,...............		......	..	150	00
1	To Merchandise, ... " 176 00					
	30th,...... 260 00		......	..	436	00
3	To Benjamin Canfield, ...18th,.............		......	..	75	00
2	SUNDRIES *Dr. to* CASH,..............		......	..	12,351	00
1	Profit and Loss, ... 4th,.............		18	95		
2	Bills Payable, ... " 3,870 00					
	9th,......1,025 00		4,895	00		
2	J. Andrews & Co......... 8th,....... 500 00					
	25th,......1,075 00		1,575	00		
1	Charges, ...15th,....... 115 05					
	30th,...... 350 00		465	05		
1	Merchandise, ...19th,.............		5,397	00		
1	MERCHANDISE *Dr. to* SUNDRIES,........		1,668	00		
3	To Bird & Beardsley, ... 1st, ...1,756 00					
	6th,...... 500 00		......	..	2,256	00
2	To J. Andrews & Co...... 8th,.......1,575 00					
	18th,...... 462 00		......	..	2,037	00
3	To William Smith,........12th,.............		......	..	375	00
1	SUNDRIES *Dr. to* MERCHANDISE,........		......	..	5,856	25
3	Thomas Harris, ... 2d,....... 205 25					
	5th,...... 457 00					
	28th,...... 164 00		826	25		
3	Benjamin Canfield,........ 8th,...... 729 00					
	15th,...... 167 00		896	00		
2	Bills Payable,............. 9th,.............		2,000	00		
4	Charles Drummond,.......20th,...... 408 00					
	29th,...... 162 00		570	00		
4	J. Thompson & Son,......25th,...... 640 00					
	30th,...... 672 00		1,312	00		
4	Edward Ford,............26th,.............		252	00		
2	BILLS RECEIVABLE *Dr. to* SUNDRIES,.....		4,770	00		
4	To Charles Drummond,.... 4th,.............		......	..	1,895	00
3	To Benjamin Canfield, ... 7th,.....		......	..	2,875	00
			34,720	25	34,720	25

Mem.— The Merchandise on hand is valued at $12,100, which, in adjusting the accounts for the purpose of balancing the Ledger, must be taken into consideration.　(See remarks, page 70.)

LEDGER.—Set 1.

INDEX.

1

Dr.		STOCK.				Cr.	
1839				1839			
Mar. 30	To Balance,..........	14,479	25	Jan. 1	By Cash, ... 1	10,000	00
				Mar. 30	By Profit and Loss,...	4,479	25
		14,479	25			14,479	25

Dr.		PROFIT AND LOSS.				Cr.	
1839				1839			
Feb. 1	To Cash,............ 2	58	75	Mar. 30	By Merchandise,......	5,377	00
" 12	To T. Harris,........ 2	130	00				
Mar. 4	To Cash,............ 3	18	95				
" 30	To Charges,.........	690	05				
	To Stock,............	4,479	25				
		5,377	00			5,377	00

Dr.		CHARGES.		•		Cr.	
1839				1839			
Jan. 10	To Cash,............ 1	150	00	Mar. 30	By Profit and Loss,...	690	05
Feb. 17	To do. 2	75	00				
Mar. 30	To do. 3	465	05				
		690	05			690	05

Dr.		MERCHANDISE.				Cr.	
1839				1839			
Jan. 3	To Cash,............ 1	1,750	00	Jan. 31	By Cash,............ 1	1,470	00
" 30	To Sundries, ... 1	12,955	00	" "	By Sundries, ... 1	9,019	50
Feb. 20	To Cash,............ 2	1,636	25	Feb. 28	By Cash,............ 2	1,772	00
" 13	To Sundries, ... 2	7,200	00	" "	By Sundries, ... 2	8,329	50
Mar. 19	To Cash,............ 3	5,397	00	Mar. 30	By Cash,............ 3	436	00
" "	To Sundries, ... 3	4,668	00	" "	By Sundries, ... 3	5,856	25
" 30	To Profit and Loss,...	5,377	00	" "	By Balance,..........	12,100	00
		38,983	25			38,983	25

2

Dr.		CASH.			Cr.

1839				1839			
Jan. 31	To Sundries,........	1	12,000 00	Jan. 28	By Sundries, ...	1	3,900 00
Feb. 28	To do.	2	7,200 00	Feb. 28	By do.	2	6,570 00
Mar. 30	To do.	3	7,075 00	Mar. 30	By do.	3	12,351 00
				" "	By Balance,..........		3,454 00
			26,275 00				26,275 00

Dr.		BILLS RECEIVABLE.			Cr.

1839				1839			
Jan. 29	To Merchandise, ...	1	1,350 00	Feb. 1	By Cash,............	2	4,820 00
Feb. 26	To do.	2	3,506 00	Mar. 30	By do.	3	6,414 00
" "	To Sundries,........	2	5,114 50	" 30	By Balance,..........		3,506 50
Mar. 7	To do.	3	4,770 00				
			14,740 50				14,740 50

Dr.		BILLS PAYABLE.			Cr.

1839				1839			
Mar. 9	To Cash,............	3	4,895 00	Jan. 30	By Merchandise,.....	1	3,870 00
" "	To Merchandise, ...	3	2,000 00	Feb. 24	By Sundries, ...	2	6,525 00
" 30	To Balance,..........		5,900 00	" 14	By Merchandise,.....	2	2,400 00
			12,795 00				12,795 00

Dr.		JAMES ANDREWS & Co.			Cr.

1839				1839			
Jan. 1	To Cash,............	1	1,500 00	Jan. 21	By Merchandise,.....	1	6,000 00
Feb. 28	To Bills Payable,....	2	4,500 00	Mar. 18	By do.	3	2,037 00
Mar. 25	To Cash,............	3	1,575 00				
" 30	To Balance,..........		462 00				
			8,037 00				8,037 00

3

Dr.	WILLIAM SMITH.				Cr.		
1839				1839			
Jan. 28	To Cash,............	1	500	00	Jan. 23	By Merchandise,.....	1	2,060	00
Feb. 14	To Bills Payable,....	2	1,000	00	Mar. 12	By do.	3	375	00
Mar. 30	To Balance, ...		935	00					
			2,435	00				2,435	00

Dr.	BIRD & BEARDSLEY.				Cr.		
1839				1839			
Feb. 24	To Bills Payable,....	2	1,025	00	Jan. 15	By Merchandise,.....	1	1,025	00
Mar. 30	To Balance,..........		2,256	00	Mar. 6	By do.	3	2,256	00
			3,281	00				3,281	00

Dr.	THOMAS HARRIS.				Cr.		
1839				1839			
Jan. 18	To Merchandise,.....	1	3,880	00	Jan. 14	By Cash,............	1	280	00
Mar. 28	To do.	3	826	25	Feb. 9	By Bills Receivable,.	2	3,470	00
					" "	By Profit and Loss, ..	2	130	00
					Mar. 12	By Cash,............	3	150	00
					" 30	By Balance,..........		676	25
			4,706	25				4,706	25

Dr.	BENJAMIN CANFIELD.				Cr.		
1839				1839			
Jan. 22	To Merchandise,.....	1	422	50	Jan. 28	By Cash,............	1	100	00
Feb. 27	To do.	2	2,875	00	Feb. 17	By Bills Receivable,.	2	322	50
Mar. 15	To do.	3	896	00	Mar. 18	By Cash,............	3	75	00
					" 7	By Bills Receivable, .	3	2,875	00
					" 30	By Balance,..........		821	00
			4,193	50				4,193	50

16   L

4

Dr.	EDWARD FORD.				Cr.

1839					1839				
Jan. 31	To Merchandise, ...	1	1,472	00	Jan. 25	By Cash,............	1	150	00
Feb. 28	To do.	2	275	00	Feb. 19	By Bills Receivable, .	2	1,322	00
" "	To do.	3	252	00	Mar. 30	*By Balance,*..........		527	00
			1,999	00				1,999	00

Dr.	CHARLES DRUMMOND.				Cr.

1839					1839				
Jan. 28	To Merchandise, ...	1	1,895	00	Mar. 4	By Bills Receivable,.	3	1,895	00
Mar. 29	To do.	3	570	00	" 30	*By Balance,*..........		570	00
			2,465	00				2,465	00

Dr.	JOHN THOMPSON & SON.				Cr.

1839					1839				
Feb. 18	To Merchandise,.....	2	1,673	50	Feb. 10	By Cash,............	2	608	00
Mar. 30	To do.	3	1,312	00	Mar. 30	*By Balance,*..........		2,377	50
			2,985	50				2,985	50

Dr.	JAMES BROWN & CO.				Cr.

1839					1839				
Feb. 28	To Cash,............	2	4,800	00	Feb. 13	By Merchandise,.....	2	4,800	00

Dr.	BALANCE.				Cr.	5

1839				1839			
Mar. 30	To Merchandise,.....	12,100	00	Mar. 30	By Bills Payable,....	5,900	00
	To Cash,............	3,454	00		By J. Andrews & Co.	462	00
	To Bills Receivable,.	3,506	50		By Wm. Smith,.....	935	00
	To T. Harris,........	676	25		By Bird & Beardsley,	2,256	00
	To B. Canfield,......	821	00		*Amount of Debts,*..	9,553	00
	To Edward Ford,....	527	00		*By Stock,*...........	14,479	25
	To C. Drummond,...	570	00				
	To J.Thompson&Son,	2,377	50				
		24,032	25			24.032	25

ANALYSIS.

Merchandise.

Am! of sales,.............26,883 25
On hand................12,100 00

Total returns,............38,983 25
Am! of purchases, ...33,606 25

Gain, on mdze,..........$5,377 00

Cash.

Am! of receipts,..........26,275 00
 " of payments, ...22,821 00

Cash, on hand,...........$3,454 00

Bills Receivable.

Am! of bills received,.....14,740 50
 "   "   disposed of,...11,234 00

Bills, on hand,...... ...$3,506 500

Bills Payable.

Am! of bills issued,.......12,795 00
 "   "   paid,......... 6,895 00

Bills, outstanding,........$5,900 00

J. Andrews & Co.

Am! received from them,....8,037 00
 " paid on account,.......7,575 00

Balance, due to J. A. & Co...$462 00

William Smith.

Am! received from.him,....2,435 00
 " paid on account,......1,500 00

Balance, due to W. S......$935 00

Bird & Beardsley.

Am! received from them, ...3,281 00
 " paid them, ...1,025 00

Balance, due to B. & B....$2,256 00

Thomas Harris.

Am! due by him,..........4,706 25
 " received from him, ...4,030 00

Balance, due by T. Harris,..$676 25

B. Canfield.

Am! due by him, ...4,193 50
 " received from him, ...3,372 50

Balance, due by B. Canfield,.$821 00

Edward Ford.

Am! due by him, ...1,999 00
 " received on account,...1,472 00

Balance, due by E. Ford, ...$527 00

C. Drummond.

Am! due by him, ...2,465 00
 " received on account, ..1,895 00

Balance, due by C. D......$570 00

J. Thompson & Son.

Am! due by them, ...2,985 50
 " received on account,.. 608 00

Balance, due by them,.....$3,377 50

1. — Capital invested,....................................10,000 00
     Net gain, to 30th March,......................... 4,479 25
                                  —————
     Present worth, or net capital,....................$14,479 25

2. — Amount of assets, 30th March,......................24,032 25
     Deduct liabilities, ... 9,553 00
                                    —————
     Present worth, as before,......................$14,479 25

See remarks on balancing, page 68, for an explanation of the foregoing statements. The entries of 'Profit and Loss,' &c., occasioned by adjusting the books, 30th March, have not been brought through the Journal, but are simply *transferred* from one account to another *in the Ledger only.* The closing entries are printed in *Italics* to distinguish them from the Journal items. The 'Trial Balance' is subjoined for the learner's assistance.

Drs.		TRIAL BALANCE. — 30th March.	Crs.	
		....................Stock,............................	10,000	00
207	70	....................Profit and Loss,.....................		
690	05	....................Charges, ...		
33,606	25	....................Merchandise,.......................	26,883	25
26,275	00	....................Cash,..............................	22,821	00
14,740	50	....................Bills Receivable,...................	11,234	00
6,895	00	....................Bills Payable,......................	12,795	00
7,575	00	....................J. Andrews & Co...................	8,037	00
1,500	00	....................William Smith,.....................	2,435	00
1,025	00	....................Bird & Beardsley, ...	3,281	00
4,706	25	....................Thomas Harris, ...	4,030	00
4,193	50	....................Benjamin Canfield,.................	3,372	50
1,999	00	....................Edward Ford,......................	1,472	00
2,465	00	....................Charles Drummond,.................	1,895	00
2,985	50	....................J. Thompson & Son,................	608	00
4,800	00	....................J. Brown & Co....................	4,800	00
113,663	75	....................*Equilibrium,*	113,663	75

The posting may be proved by adding together the several transactions for each month ; the *total* of which, if the books are correctly adjusted, will agree with the total of the 'Trial Balance.' The transactions, agreeably to the footings of the *Journal,* are as follows : —

JANUARY,...........(see Journal, page 114,).............37,874 50
FEBRUARY,..........(" " " 115,)..............41,069 00
MARCH,............(" " " 116,)............. 34,720 25
                                    —————
     Total,..113,663 75

When the book-keeper has completed his 'Trial Balance,' it is within the range of possibilities that the Debits and Credits may amount to the same sum. But, if they should happen to do so, what then? Does that agreement prove the correctness of his books? Certainly not. The utmost it shows is, that the *Dr.* and *Cr.* sides of the *Ledger* are equal in amount. There may still exist errors of additions, or omissions of items, on both sides, made either by accident or for the express purpose of deception, to an unknown extent. But suppose the aggregate amounts should not agree; in what a situation is the book-keeper placed! He has no clew to the error, although he is convinced that it exists; and, not knowing the real amount, he cannot tell which side of the Ledger to examine, or whether the errors — for there may be several — are in the Journal entries, or whether they are in the postings, additions, or subtractions. Thus circumstanced, he has the twelve months' work to examine. He may call over the postings, add up every account, and reëxamine the whole, and perhaps find, as he proceeds, several mistakes, sometimes making the difference larger, and sometimes smaller, and, after all his anxiety and labor, leave off with his 'Trial Balance' evidently in error. By this process of balancing, weeks, and often months, are spent in tiresome examinations for the detection of errors.

The above check, however, will detect any omission in *posting;* and, if a mistake has been made, it leads to an easy discovery of it. As the two sides of the Ledger, when added, will agree with each other, if correct, and as the total amount of the several transactions will correspond with each side of the 'Trial Balance, or, in case of an error, with that side which is correct, this check points out where the error lies, and, of course, directs the book-keeper's search in examining the books.

L *

SET II.

MERCHANTS' ACCOUNTS

EXEMPLIFIED IN THE BOOKS OF

REED, JONES, & CO.,

GENERAL MERCHANTS, NEW YORK.

PRELIMINARY REMARKS.

It will be observed, that the entries in the Day Book, Set II., are expressed in the Journal form, the debtors and creditors being pointed out in the first instance. This practice is now very generally adopted by accountants, and it is certainly preferable to that of making the entries in common language.

It is customary, in real business, to transfer the items directly from the Subsidiary Books to the Journal, as exemplified in Chapter IV.; but, in teaching, this method has been found very inconvenient; and therefore, in the following arrangement, every transaction, except the cash received and paid, is recorded in the Day Book.

Instead of debiting '*Charges*' for the money paid upon goods consigned to us for sale, an account, entitled '*Consignments,*' is debited for all such disbursements, and credited for the same when the sales are adjusted. It will also be seen that, in Set II., we have opened only one account in the Ledger for the goods sold on commission, under the title of '*Sales of Consignments,*' which is credited for the sales as they occur, and debited for the net proceeds and all charges which may have been incurred on any individual consignment. The particulars of each consignment are recorded in the *Sales Book,* as described at page 43. (See Remarks, page 24.)

CASH BOOK.—Set II.

17

1 *Dr.*	CASH.		
1839	Balance, in hand,........	20,000	00
July 2	To Stephen Homer, ...received from him,.......	1,000	00
" 15	To James Forbes.,.... " " "	300	00
" 27	To Wm. Harris,...... " " "	500	00
" 31	To Merchandise,...... " for sales,.......	363	64
" "	To Bills Receivable,... " No. 10,........	5,000	00
		27,163	64
	Ent^d Journal, fol. 2.		
Aug. 1	Balance, from July, ...	10,141	00
" 10	To Bills Receivable,...received No. 11,........	3,750	00
" 14	To Stephen Homer, ... " in full, ...	2,850	00
" 18	To Ship Nero,........ " for freight,......	3,000	00
" 27	To Bills Receivable,... " No. 12,........	1,250	00
		20,991	00
	Ent^d Journal, fol. 4.		
Sept.	Balance, from August,....	4,619	60
" 1	To Bills Receivable,...received No. 15,........	1,150	00
" 7	To City Bank,........℗ order,...............	5,000	00
" 10	To Ship Nero,........received for freight,......	300	00
" 13	To City Bank,........℗ order,...............	6,000	00
" 24	To " " ....for Cotton,.............	5,250	00
" 28	To Fenn & Park, ...rec^d in full,...........	68	70
" "	To Merchandise,...... " drawback on Sugar,..	4,329	60
		26,717	90
	Ent^d Journal, fol. 6.		

	CONTRA.		Cr.

1839			
July 3	By City Bank, ...deposited this day,......	15,000	00
" 15	By Charges,..........℔ Petty Cash Book,......	332	64
" 18	By Ship Nero,......,...for insurance, &c.......	100	00
" 25	By Bills Payable,......paid No. 7,.............	1,500	00
" 31	By Charges,..........stationery, &c...........	90	00
	Balance, to August,......	10,141	00
		27,163	64

Entᵈ Journal, fol. 2.

Aug. 1	By Bills Payable, ...paid No. 8, ...	2,700	00
" 10	By John Ramsay,..... " in full,.............	2,000	00
" 17	By William Irving,.... " on account,........	1,000	00
" "	By Charges,.......... " ℔ Petty Cash Book,..	543	40
" 24	By Bills Payable, ... " No. 12,.............	4,478	00
" "	By City Bank,........deposited, ...	5,500	00
" 31	By Thomas Jones, ...personal expenses,.......	150	00
	Balance, to September,...	4,619	60
		20,991	00

Entᵈ Journal, fol. 4.

Sept. 7	By Charges,.,.........on shipment ℔ Aurora, ...	203	28
" 8	By Consignments,.....freight, &c., ℔ Cuba, ...	1,361	62
" 10	By Hope Insurance Co..for insurance, &c.......	338	28
" "	By Bills Payable,......paid No. 9,.............	800	00
" 16	By John Reed,.......̈.personal expenses,.......	500	00
" 17	By Consignments,.....duties, &c., ℔ Cuba,.....	4,600	00
" "	By Bills Payable,......paid No. 13, ...	3,625	00
" 20	By Ship Nero,........ " for repairs, &c......	800	00
23	By Charges,.......... " rent, &c...........	500	00
" 24	By Cotton,........... " for 100 bales,.......	5,250	00
" 29	By Hope Insurance Co. " in full, ...	318	40
	Balance, on hand,........	8,421	32
		26,717	90

Entᵈ Journal, fol. 6.

DAY BOOK.—Set II.

1

NEW YORK, *July* 1, 1839.

	Inventory of the Assets and Liabilities of Reed, Jones, & Co., as ℣ 'Balance Sheet,' 30th June.		
	ASSETS.		
	Cash,................balance in hand,............	20,000	00
	Bills Receivable,...... ″ ″ ″	15,000	00
1	Ship Nero,...........valued at...................	10,000	00
	Merchandise,.......... ″	8,000	00
	Stephen Homer ....owes us...................	5,000	00
	William Harris .... ″	3,000	00
	James Forbes......... ″	1,500	00
	Amount of our assets,...........	62,500	00
	LIABILITIES.		
	Bills Payable,.........outstanding,...............	5,000	00
	John Ramsay,.........due to him,...............	3,500	00
1	William Irving,........ ″	2,300	00
	Thomas Ryder,........ ″	1,700	00
	Amount of our liabilities,........	12,500	00
	—————— 10 ——————		
1	INSURANCE *Dr. to Hope Insurance Co.*		
	For Premium and Policy on Goods ℣ Neptune for New Orleans, ...	39	86
	—————— 12 ——————		
1	BILLS RECEIVABLE *Dr. to Stephen Homer,*		
	For Draft on Holmes & Son, No. 15,..............	1,150	00
	—————— 15 ——————		
1	ADVENTURE TO NEW ORLEANS *Dr. to Sundries,*		
	For Invoice of Goods ℣ Neptune, consigned for sale to R. Mason, on our account and risk, as ℣ I. B.		
	To Merchandise, ...1,972 96		
	To Charges, ... 80 18		
	To Insurance, ... 39 86	2,093	00
	—————— 25 ——————		
1	INSURANCE *Dr. to Hope Insurance Co.*		
	For Premium and Policy on Produce consigned to us ℣ Cuba, from Jamaica, ℣ S. B................	195	12

		2
NEW YORK, *July* 27, 1839.		

1	BILLS RECEIVABLE *Dr. to James Forbes,* For his Draft on James Benson & Sons, No. 16,......	1,000	00

30

2	COTTON *Dr. to Sundries,* For Invoice of 100 bales, ℔ Ann, from New Orleans, To Robert Mason, for amount of Invoice, ...5,610 00 To Hope Ins. Co. for Insurance, &c......... 86 75	5,696	75

31

2	SUNDRIES *Dr. to Bills Payable,* For the following Bills, accepted this day, viz. Murray & Co....No. 10, at 60 days' sight,...2,400 00 John Ramsay,....No. 11, at 90 *"* date,....1,500 00	3,900	00

AUGUST 1, 1839.

3	BILLS RECEIVABLE *Dr. to J. Stirling,* For Draft on Lloyd & Co., at 60 days' sight, No. 17,..	500	00

5

3	INSURANCE *Dr. to Hope Insurance Co.* For Premium on shipment ℔ Isabella for Jamaica, $6,720, at 1½ ℔ cent, and Policies, $2 50,........	103	30

"

3	SUNDRIES *Dr. to Sundries,* For Goods shipped ℔ the Isabella for Jamaica, by order and for account of the following persons, as ℔ I. B. — *Drs.* — John Stirling, for Goods,..........amounting to...........2,024 40 Charges........paid at shipping,........ 158 12 Commission......on Goods, &c............ 67 50 Insurance........on $2,400, and Policy, ... 37 25	2,287	27
	Murray & Co., for Goods,..........amounting to...........3,639 00 Charges.........paid at shipping,........ 227 16 Commission......on Goods, &c........... 120 00 Insurance........on $4,320, and Policy, ... 66 05	4,052	21
	— *Crs.* —	6,339	48
	To Merchandise, ...as above,...........5,663 40 To Charges, ... *"* .... 385 28 To Commission,........ *"* .... 187 50 To Insurance,.......... *"* 103 30		
	$6,339 48		

3	New York, *August* 11, 1839.		
3	INDIGO IN Co. *Dr. to Bills Payable,* For 16 chests Bengal Indigo, purchased on joint account with J. Ramsay, for which we have given our Note, at 10 days' date, No. 12,..............	4,478	00
	——— 17 ———		
3	BILLS RECEIVABLE *Dr. to William Harris,* For his Draft in our favor on Sylvester & Co., No. 18,	2,500	00
	——— 15 ———		
3	ROBERT MASON *Dr. to Bills Payable,* For our Acceptance in favor Taylor, No. 13,........	3,625	00
	——— 25 ———		
3	STEPHEN HOMER *Dr. to Indigo in Co.* For 16 chests Bengal Indigo, 1,696 lb. net, @ $3,.....	5,088	00
	——— 30 ———		
3	R. MASON *Dr. to Adventure to New Orleans,* For net proceeds of Goods consigned to him ℔ Neptune,	2,600	00
	——— 31 ———		
4	INDIGO IN Co. *Dr. to Sundries,* For the following, to close that account, as ℔ S. B. To Commission.,.....for 2½ ℔ cent on sales,....127 20 To John Ramsay,...for his ½ net gain,.......241 40 To Profit and Loss,..for our ½ ″ ″ 241 40	610	00
	——— ″ ———		
4	SUNDRIES *Dr. to Cotton,* For sales of 100 bales, ℔ the Ann, as follows : — E. Robinson,....25 bales, 8,526 lb. net,....@ 20 cts. W. Harris,......50 ″ 17,210 lb. net,....@ 20 cts. J. Forbes, ...25 ″ 8,630 lb. net,....@ 20 cts.	1,705 3,442 1,726 —— 6,873	20 00 00 —— 20
	——— SEPTEMBER 1, 1839. ———		
5	MERCHANDISE *Dr. to James Thompson,* For 30 hhds. refined Sugar, amounting, ℔ B. P., to....	12,000	00
	——— 5 ———		
5	MERCHANDISE *Dr. to William Irving,* For 10 hhds. refined Sugar, amounting, ℔ B. P., to....	2,928	40

		4
	NEW YORK, *September* 6, 1839.	

5	INSURANCE *Dr. to Hope Insurance Co.* For Premium on $11,520, at 2 ℔ cent, on Sugar, ℔ the Aurora, for Rotterdam, and Policy, $1 25,.......	231	65
	———— 7 ————		
5	SUNDRIES *Dr. to Sundries,* For amount of 40 hhds. refined Sugar, shipped ℔ the Aurora for Rotterdam, as ℔ I. B. — *Drs.* — John Ramsay,...........his ⅓,............3,785 43 Vanderpoole & Co.......their ⅓, ...3,785 43 Adventure to Rotterdam,..our ⅓, ...3,785 44	11,356	30
5	— *Crs.* — To Merchandise,...for cost, (less drawback,). 10,598 80 To Charges,......paid at shipping, ... 203 28 To Insurance, ...as above,.............. 231 65 To Commission,...on cost, &c............ 322 57 $11,356 30		
	———— 8 ————		
5	WILLIAM IRVING *Dr. to Bills Payable,* For our Acceptance in favor of Hill, No. 14,.........	1,900	00
	———— 10 ————		
5	BILLS RECEIVABLE *Dr. to Vanderpoole & Co.* For Bill on Prime, Ward, & King, at 60 days' sight, No. 19,..................................	2,500	00
	———— 12 ————		
5	JAMES THOMPSON *Dr. to Bills Payable,* For our Acceptance, at 10 days' sight, No. 15, ...	4,800	00
	———— 13 ————		
6	FENN & PARK *Dr. to Sales of Consignments,* For 30 hhds. Rum, ℔ Cuba, ℔ Sales Book, ...	3,668	70
	———— 15 ————		
5	BILLS RECEIVABLE *Dr. to E. Robinson,* For his Acceptance, at 30 days' date, No. 20,........	1,000	00
	———— 18 ————		
5	JAMES THOMPSON *Dr. to Bills Receivable,* For Bill No. 19, endorsed to him, ...	2,500	00

18   M *

5	NEW YORK, *September* 20, 1839.		
5	BILLS RECEIVABLE *Dr. to W. Harris,* For his Acceptance, at 30 days' date, No. 21, ...	3,000	00
	— 23 —		
6	JAMES THOMPSON *Dr. to Sales of Consignments,* For 10 hhds. Sugar, 131 cwt. 0 qrs. 14 lbs., at $20 ℔ cwt.	2,622	50
	— 24 —		
5	BILLS RECEIVABLE *Dr. to James Forbes,* For his Acceptance, at 30 days' date, No. 22, ...	1,726	00
	— 25 —		
6	THOMAS ATWOOD & CO. *Dr. to Sales of Consignments,* For 30 hhds. Sugar, 378 cwt. net, at $20 ℔ cwt......	7,560	00
	— 26 —		
6	DAWSON & SONS *Dr. to Sales of Consignments,* For 10 tierces Coffee, 60 cwt. 2 qrs. at $30 48 ℔ cwt..	1,844	04
	— 27 —		
5	BILLS RECEIVABLE *Dr. to Fenn & Park,* For their Acceptance, at 30 days' date, No. 23, ...	3,600	00
	— 28 —		
6	JAMES BROWN & CO. *Dr. to Sales of Consignments,* For 40 planks Mahogany, 1,344 feet, @ 50 cts.......	672	00
	— 30 —		

6	SALES OF CONSIGNMENTS *Dr. to Sundries,*
	For adjustment of sales Produce ℔ Cuba, ℔ S. B.
	To Insurance,......Premium and Policies,..........
	To Consignments, ..Duty, Freight, &c.............
	To Commission, ...on Sales and Insurance,........
	To John Stirling,...net proceeds of
	  30 hhds. Rum,......................3,071 80
	  10 ″ Sugar,......................1,411 10
	To Murray & Co....for net proceeds of
	  30 hhds. Sugar,......................3,824 31
	  10 tierces Coffee,....................1,108 86
	  40 planks Mahogany,................ 381 33
		195
		5,961
		413
		
		4,482
		
		5,314
		—————
		16,367
			12
			62
			10
			
			90
			
			50
			———
			24

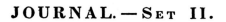

JOURNAL. — Set II.

	JULY, 1839.	— Drs. —		— Crs. —	
1					
1	SUNDRIES *Dr. to* STOCK,.................	.....	..	62,500	00
	For the following Assets, as ℔ Balance Sheet, 30th June : —				
4	Cash,.....................................	20,000	00		
4	Bills Receivable,...........................	15,000	00		
2	Ship Nero,.................................	10,000	00		
2	Merchandise,..............................	8,000	00		
5	Stephen Homer,...........................	5,000	00		
5	William Harris,............................	3,000	00		
5	James Forbes,.............................	1,500	00		
1	STOCK *Dr. to* SUNDRIES,..................	12,500	00		
	For Liabilities, as ℔ Balance Sheet, 30th June.				
4	To Bills Payable,...........................	.....	..	5,000	00
5	To John Ramsay,...........................	.....	..	3,500	00
6	To William Irving,.........................	.....	..	2,300	00
6	To Thomas Ryder,.........................	.....	..	1,700	00
1 / 6	INSURANCE *Dr. to* HOPE INSURANCE CO.....	234	98		
	For the following Insurances, effected this month : —				
	On Goods ℔ Neptune, ...10th,...... 39 86				
	On Produce ℔ Cuba, ...25th,......195 12	.....	..	234	98
4	BILLS RECEIVABLE *Dr. to* SUNDRIES,......	2,150	00		
	For Bills received this month.				
5	To Stephen Homer, ...12th,..............	.....	..	1,150	00
5	To James Forbes, ...27th,..............	.....	..	1,000	00
3	ADVENTURE TO NEW ORLEANS *Dr. to* SUNDRIES,	2,093	00		
	For shipment ℔ Neptune, ℔ I. B., 15th inst.				
2	To Merchandise,............................	.....	..	1,972	96
2	To Charges,................................	.....	..	80	18
1	To Insurance,..............................	.....	..	39	86
	Forward,..............	79,477	98	79,477	98

		— Drs. —		— Crs. —	
	JULY, 1839.			**2**	
	Am! bro!. forward,........	79,477	98	79,477	98
3	COTTON *Dr. to* SUNDRIES,..............	5,696	75		
	For cost of 100 bales, ℔ Ann, 30th.				
6	To Robert Mason,......................	......	..	5,610	00
6	To Hope Insurance Co....................	......	..	86	75
4	SUNDRIES *Dr. to* BILLS PAYABLE,........	......	..	3,900	00
	For Bills accepted 31st inst.				
7	Murray & Co.............................	2,400	00		
5	John Ramsay,...........................	1,500	00		
4	CASH *Dr. to* SUNDRIES,..................	7,163	64		
	Received this month, ℔ Cash Book.				
5	To Stephen Homer,....... 2d, ...	......	..	1,000	00
5	To James Forbes, ...15th,............	......	..	300	00
5	To William Harris,.......27th,............	......	..	500	00
2	To Merchandise, ...31st,............	......	..	363	64
4	To Bills Receivable,....... "	......	..	5,000	00
4	SUNDRIES *Dr. to* CASH,..................	......	..	17,022	64
	Paid this month, ℔ Cash Book.				
7	City Bank,............... 3d, ...	15,000	00		
2	Charges, ...15th,........332 64				
	31st,........ 90 00	422	64		
2	Ship Nero, ...18th,.............	100	00		
4	Bills Payable,...........25th,.............	1,500	00		
		113,261	01	113,261	01

3	AUGUST, 1839.				
		— Drs. —		— Crs. —	
4	BILLS RECEIVABLE *Dr. to* SUNDRIES,.......	3,000	00		
	Received this month.				
7	To John Stirling, ...1st,..............	.....	..	500	00
5	To William Harris,.......17th,..............	.....	..	2,500	00
$\frac{1}{6}$	INSURANCE *Dr. to* HOPE INSURANCE Co.....	103	30		
	For Insurance, &c., on Goods ℔ Isabella, 5th,...	.....	..	103	30
	SUNDRIES *Dr. to* SUNDRIES,				
	For shipment ℔ Isabella, 5th inst., for Jamaica.				
	— Drs. —				
7	John Stirling,..............................	2,287	27		
7	Murray & Co..............................	4,052	21		
	— Crs. —				
2	To Merchandise,..........................	.....	..	5,663	40
2	To Charges, ...	.....	..	385	28
1	To Commission, ...	.....	..	187	50
1	To Insurance,...........................	.....	..	103	30
4	SUNDRIES *Dr. to* BILLS PAYABLE,..........	.....	..	8,103	00
	Accepted this month				
3	Indigo in Co.............11th,..............	4,478	00		
6	Robert Mason,..........15th,..............	3,625	00		
$\frac{5}{3}$	STEPHEN HOMER *Dr. to* INDIGO IN Co......	5,088	00		
	For 16 chests Bengal,.......`.25th,............	.....	..	5,088	00
$\frac{6}{3}$	R. MASON *Dr. to* ADVENTURE TO N. ORLEANS,	2,600	00		
	For net proceeds of Goods ℔ Neptune, 30th,....	.....	..	2,600	00
	Forward,..............	25,233	78	25,233	78

	AUGUST, 1839.			4	
		— Drs. —		— Crs. —	
	Amt. broᵗ forward,........	25,233	78	25,233	78
3	INDIGO IN Co. *Dr. to* SUNDRIES,..........	610	00		
	For adjustment of that account.				
1	To Commission,...........31st...............	......	..	127	20
5	To John Ramsay,......... "	......	..	241	40
1	To Profit and Loss,........ "	......	..	241	40
3	SUNDRIES *Dr. to* COTTON, ...	......	..	6,873	20
	For sales 100 bales ℔ Ann, 31st inst.				
7	Edward Robinson,...........................	1,705	20		
5	William Harris, ...	3,442	00		
5	James Forbes,...............................	1,726	00		
4	CASH *Dr. to* SUNDRIES,.................	10,850	00		
	Received this month, ℔ Cash Book				
4	To Bills Receivable,......10th,......3,750 00				
	27th,......1,250 00	......	..	5,000	00
5	To Stephen Homer,.......14th,...............	......	..	2,850	00
2	To ship Nero,...........18th,...............	......	..	3,000	00
4	SUNDRIES *Dr. to* CASH,.................	......	..	16,371	40
	Paid this month, ℔ Cash Book.				
4	Bills Payable, ... 1st, ...2,700 00				
	24th,......4,478 00	7,178	00		
5	John Ramsay,............10th,...............	2,000	00		
6	William Irving, ...17th,...............	1,000	00		
2	Charges,.................. "	543	40		
7	City Bank, ...24th,...............	5,500	00		
8	Thomas Jones,...........31st,...............	150	00		
		59,938	38	59,938	38

5	SEPTEMBER, 1839.	— Drs. —		— Crs. —	
2	MERCHANDISE Dr. to SUNDRIES,...........	14,928	40		
	For 40 hhds. refined Sugar, ⅌ B. P.				
8	To James Thompson,.......1st,..............	......	..	12,000	00
6	To William Irving, ...5th,.............	......	..	2,928	40
1 — 6	INSURANCE Dr. to HOPE INSURANCE CO.....	231	65		
	For Premium and Policy on Sugar, ⅌ Aurora, 6th,	......	..	231	65
	SUNDRIES Dr. to SUNDRIES,				
	For shipment to Rotterdam ⅌ Aurora, ⅌ I. B.				
	— Drs. —				
5	John Ramsay,..............7th,.............	3,785	43		
8	Vanderpoole & Co......... "	3,785	43		
3	Adventure to Rotterdam,.... "	3,785	44		
	— Crs. —				
2	To Merchandise,...........................	......	..	10,598	80
2	To Charges, ...	......	..	203	28
1	To Insurance, ...	......	..	231	65
1	To Commission, ...·..	......	..	322	57
4	SUNDRIES Dr. to BILLS PAYABLE,.....	......	..	6,100	00
	Accepted this month.				
6	William Irving, ... 8th,..............	1,300	00		
8	James Thompson, ...12th,.............	4,800	00		
4	BILLS RECEIVABLE Dr. to SUNDRIES,.......	11,826	00		
	Received this month.				
8	To Vanderpoole & Co.....10th,.............	......	..	2,500	00
7	To E. Robinson,..........15th,.............	......	..	1,000	00
5	To William Harris, ...20th,.............	......	..	3,000	00
5	To James Forbes, ...24th,.............	......	..	1,726	00
9	To Fenn & Park,.........27th,.............	......	..	3,600	00
8 — 4	JAMES THOMPSON Dr. to BILLS RECEIVABLE,	2,500	00		
	For Bill No. 19, endorsed to him,.............	......	..	2,500	00
	Forward,..............	46,942	35	46,942	35

SEPTEMBER, 1839.

6

		— Drs —	— Crs —
	Am'. bro'. forward,........	46,942|35	46,942|35
4	SUNDRIES *Dr. to* SALES OF CONSIGNMENTS,..	......|..	16,367|24
	For sales of Produce ⅌ Cuba.		
9	Fenn & Park,...........13th,.............	3,668|70	
8	James Thompson,........23d, ...	2,622|50	
9	Thomas Atwood & Co.....25th,.............	7,560|00	
9	Dawson & Sons,..........26th,.............	1,844|04	
9	James Brown & Co.......28th,.............	672|00	
4	SALES OF CONSIGNMENTS *Dr. to* SUNDRIES,..	16,367|24	
	For adjustment of sales ⅌ Cuba, ⅌ S. B.		
1	To Insurance,...........30th,.............	.....	195|12
2	To Consignments, ... "	.....	5,961|62
1	To Commission, ... "	.....	413|10
7	To John Stirling, ... "	.....	4,482|90
7	To Murray & Co......... "	.....	5,314|50
4	CASH *Dr. to* SUNDRIES,...................	22,098|30	
	Received this month, ⅌ Cash Book.		
4	To Bills Receivable,...... 1st,.............	......|..	1,150|00
7	To City Bank, ... 7th,......5,000 00		
	13th,......6,000 00		
	24th,......5,250 00	......|..	16,250|00
2	To Ship Nero,..........10th,.............	......|..	300|00
9	To Fenn & Park, ...28th,.............	......|..	68|70
2	To Merchandise, ... "	......|..	4,329|60
4	SUNDRIES *Dr. to* CASH,...................	......|..	18,296|58
	Paid this month, ⅌ Cash Book.		
2	Charges,................ 7th, ... 203 28		
	23d, ... 500 00	703|28	
2	Consignments, ... 8th, ...1,361 62		
	17th, ...4,600 00	5,961|62	
6	Hope Insurance Co........10th, ... 338 28		
	29th, ... 318 40	656|68	
4	Bills Payable,............10th, ... 800 00		
	17th, ...3,625 00	4,425|00	
8	John Reed, ...16th,.............	500|00	
2	Ship Nero,...............20th,.............	800|00	
3	Cotton,..................24th,.............	5,250|00	
	Forward,.............	120,071|71	120,071|71

19

N

7	SEPTEMBER, 1839.				
		— *Drs.* —		— *Crs.* —	
	Am^t bro^t. forward,........	120,071	71	120,071	71
1	SUNDRIES *Dr. to* PROFIT AND LOSS,......	......	..	7,133	82
	For gain on the following Accounts to 30th inst.				
1	Commission,................................	1,050	37		
2	Ship Nero,................................	4,400	00		
3	Adventure to New Orleans,..................	507	00		
3	Cotton,....................................	1,176	45		
1	PROFIT AND LOSS *Dr. to* SUNDRIES,......	7,375	22		
	To close the following Accounts to 30th inst.				
2	To Charges,................................	......	..	1,000	58
1	To Stock,..................................	......	..	6,374	64
9	BALANCE *Dr. to* SUNDRIES,..............	75,776	17		
	For closing all Accounts which balance in our favor to 30th inst.				
2	To Ship Nero,.............................	......	..	12,000	00
3	To Cotton,.................................	......	..	5,250	00
3	To Adventure to Rotterdam,.................	......	..	3,785	44
4	To Cash, ...	......	..	8,421	32
4	To Bills Receivable,........................	......	..	18,326	00
5	To Stephen Homer,.........................	......	..	5,088	00
5	To William Harris, ...	......	..	442	00
5	To James Forbes,..........................	......	..	200	00
5	To John Ramsay,..........................	......	..	3,544	03
6	To Robert Mason,..........................	......	..	615	00
7	To Murray & Co............................	......	..	1,137	71
7	To City Bank,.............................	......	..	4,250	00
7	To Edward Robinson,.......................	......	..	705	20
8	To Thomas Jones, ...	......	..	150	00
8	To John Reed, ...	......	..	500	00
8	To Vanderpoole & Co.......................	......	..	1,285	43
9	To Thomas Atwood & Co....................	......	..	7,560	00
9	To Dawson & Sons, ...	......	..	1,844	04
9	To James Brown & Co......................	......	..	672	00
9	SUNDRIES *Dr. to* BALANCE,..............	......	..	75,776	17
	For closing all Accounts wherein the Balances are against us.				
4	Bills Payable,..............................	10,000	00		
6	William Irving, ...	2,928	40		
6	Thomas Ryder,.............................	1,700	00		
7	John Stirling,..............................	2,695	63		
8	James Thompson,..........................	2,077	50		
1	Stock,.....................................	56,374	64		
		286,133	09	286,133	09

LEDGER.—Set II.

INDEX.

Dr.	STOCK.						*Cr.*		1
1839					1839				
July 1	To Sundries,........	1	12,500	00	July 1	By Sundries,........	1	62,500	00
Sep. 30	To Balance,.........	7	56,374	64	Sep. 30	By Profit and Loss,..	7	6,374	64
			68,874	64				68,874	64
						68,874 64			
						12,500 00			
						56,374 64			

Dr.	PROFIT AND LOSS.							*Cr.*	
1839					1839				
Sep. 30	To Sundries,........	7	7,375	22	Aug.31	By Indigo in Co.....	4	241	40
					Sep. 30	By Sundries, ...	7	7,133	82
			7,375	22				7 375	22

Dr.	COMMISSION.							*Cr.*	
1839					1839				
Sep. 30	To Profit and Loss,..	7	1,050	37	Aug. 5	By Sundries,........	3	187	50
					" 31	By Indigo in Co.....	4	127	20
					Sep. 7	By Sundries, ...	5	322	57
					" 30	By Sales of Consign's,	6	413	10
			1,050	37				1,050	37

Dr.	INSURANCE.							*Cr.*	
1839					1839				
July 1	To Hope Ins Co.....	1	234	98	July 15	By Adven. to N. Orl.	1	39	86
Aug. 5	To do.	3	103	30	Aug. 5	By Sundries, ...	3	103	30
Sep. 6	To do.	5	231	65	Sep. 6	By do.	5	231	65
					" 30	By Sales of Consign's,	6	195	12
			569	93				569	93

N*

2

Dr.   M E R C H A N D I S E .   **Cr.**

1839					1839				
July 1	To Stock............	1	8,000	00	July 15	By Adven. to N. Orl.	1	1,972	96
Sep. 5	To Sundries,........	5	14,928	40	" 31	By Cash,.............	2	363	64
					Aug. 5	By Sundries, ...	3	5,663	40
					Sep. 7	By do.	5	10,598	80
					" 30	By Cash, ...	6	4,329	60
			22,928	40				22,928	40

Dr.   S H I P   N E R O .   **Cr.**

1839					1839				
July 1	To Stock,............	1	10,000	00	Aug.18	By Cash,............	4	3,000	00
" 18	To Cash,.............	2	100	00	Sep. 10	By do.	6	300	00
Sep. 20	To do.	6	800	00	" 30	By Balance,.........	7	12,000	00
" 30	To Profit and Loss,..	7	4,400	00					
			15,300	00				15,300	00

Dr.   C H A R G E S .   **Cr.**

1839					1839				
July 15	To Cash,............	2	422	64	July 15	By Adven. to N. Orl.	1	80	18
Aug.17	To do.	4	543	40	Aug. 5	By Sundries,........	3	385	28
Sep. 23	To do.	6	703	28	Sep. 7	By do.	5	203	28
					" 30	By Profit and Loss,..	7	1,000	58
			1,669	32				1,669	32

Dr.   C O N S I G N M E N T S .   **Cr.**

1839					1839				
Sep. 17	To Cash,............	6	5,961	62	Sep. 30	By Sales of Consign's,	6	5,961	62

3

Dr.			COTTON.					Cr.		
1839					1839					
July 30	To Sundries,........	2	5,696	75	Aug. 31	By Sundries,........	4	6,873	20
Sep. 24	To Cash,............	6	5,250	00	Sep. 30	By Balance,........	7	5,250	00
	To Profit and Loss,..	7	1,176	45						
			12,123	20				12,123	20

12,123 20
10,946 75
————
1,176 45

Dr.			INDIGO IN CO.					Cr.		
1839					1839					
Aug.11	To Bills Payable,....	3	4,478	00	Aug.25	By S. Homer, ...	3	5,088	00
" 31	To Sundries,........	4	610	00						
			5,088	00				5,088	00

Dr.			ADVENTURE TO NEW ORLEANS.					Cr.		
1839					1839					
July 15	To Sundries,........	1	2,093	00	Aug. 30	By R. Mason,........	3	2,600	00
Sep. 30	To Profit and Loss,..	7	507	00						
			2,600	00				2,600	00

2,600 00
2,093 00
————
507 00

Dr.			ADVENTURE TO ROTTERDAM.					Cr.		
1839					1839					
Sep. 7	To Sundries,........	5	3,785	44	Sep. 30	By Balance, ...	7	3,785	44

4

Dr.	SALES OF CONSIGNMENTS.							Cr.

1839					1839				
Sep. 30	To Sundries,........	6	16,367	24	Sep. 30	By Sundries, ...	6	16,367	24

Dr.	CASH.							Cr.

1839					1839				
July 1	To Stock,..........	1	20,000	00	July 31	By Sundries,........	2	17,022	64
" 31	To Sundries,........	2	7,163	64	Aug.31	By do.	4	16,371	40
Aug.31	To do.	4	10,850	00	Sep. 30	By do.	6	18,296	58
Sep. 30	To do.	6	22,098	30		By Balance,........	7	8,421	32
			60,111	94				60,111	94

```
60,111 94
51,690 62
————————
 8,421 32
```

Dr.	BILLS RECEIVABLE.							Cr.

1839					1839				
July 1	To Stock,..........	1	15,000	00	July 31	By Cash,............	2	5,000	00
" 27	To Sundries,........	1	2,150	00	Aug.27	By do.	4	5,000	00
Aug.17	To do.	3	3,000	00	Sept.	By James Thompson,	5	2,500	00
Sep.27	To do.	5	11,826	00	" 1	By Cash,............	6	1,150	00
					" 30	By Balance,........	7	18,326	00
			31,976	00				31,976	00

```
31,976 00
13,650 00
————————
18,326 00
```

Dr.	BILLS PAYABLE.							Cr.

1839					1839				
July 25	To Cash,............	2	1,500	00	July 1	By Stock,............	1	5,000	00
Aug.24	To do.	4	7,178	00	" 31	By Sundries,........	2	3,900	00
Sep. 17	To do.	6	4,425	00	Aug.31	By do.	3	8,103	00
" 30	To Balance, ...	7	10,000	00	Sep. 31	By do.	5	6,100	00
			23,103	00				23,103	00

```
23,103 00
13,103 00
————————
10,000 00
```

5

Dr.					STEPHEN HOMER.			*Cr.*	
1839					1839				
July 1	To Stock,...........	1	5,000	00	July 12	By Bills Receivable,.	1	1,150	00
Aug.25	To Indigo in Co.....	3	5,088	00	" 2	By Cash,...........	2	1,000	00
					Aug.14	By do.	4	2,850	00
					Sep. 30	By Balance,........	7	5,088	00
			10,088	00				10,088	00

10,088 00
5,000 00
——————
5,088 00

Dr.					WILLIAM HARRIS.			*Cr.*	
1839					1839				
July 1	To Stock,...........	1	3,000	00	July 27	By Cash,...........	2	500	00
Aug.31	To Cotton,..........	4	3,442	00	Aug 17	By Bills Receivable,.	3	2,500	00
					Sep. 20	By do.	5	3,000	00
					" 30	By Balance,........	7	442	00
			6,442	00				6,442	00

6,442 00
6,000 00
——————
442 00

Dr.					JAMES FORBES.			*Cr.*	
1839					1839				
July 1	To Stock,...........	1	1,500	00	July 27	By Bills Receivable, .	1	1,000	00
Aug.31	To Cotton,..........	4	1,726	00	" 15	By Cash,...........	2	300	00
					Sep. 24	By Bills Receivable,.	5	1,726	00
					" 30	By Balance,........	7	200	00
			3,226	00				3,226	00

3,226 00
3,026 00
——————
200 00

Dr.					JOHN RAMSAY.			*Cr.*	
1839					1839				
July 31	To Bills Payable,....	2	1,500	00	July 1	By Stock,...........	1	3,500	00
Aug.10	To Cash,...........	4	2,000	00	Aug.31	By Indigo in Co.....	3	241	40
Sep. 7	To Sundries,........	5	3,785	43	Sep. 30	By Balance,........	7	3,544	03
			7,285	43				7,285	43

7,285 43
3,741 40
——————
3,544 03

20

6

Dr.			WILLIAM IRVING.				Cr.

1839					1839						
Aug. 17	To Cash,............	4	1,000	00	July 1	By Stock,...........	1	2,300	00
Sep. 8	To Bills Payable,....	5	1,300	00	Sep. 5	By Merchandise,.....	5	2,928	40
" 30	To Balance,.........	7	2,928	40					
			5,228	40				5,228	40
						5,228 40			
						2,300 00			
						2,928 40			

Dr.			THOMAS RYDER.				Cr.

1839					1839				
Sep. 30	To Balance,.........	7	1,700	00	July 1	By Stock,...........	1	1,700	00

Dr.			HOPE INSURANCE CO.				Cr.

1839					1839				
Sep. 29	To Cash,............	6	656	68	July 25	By Insurance,.......	1	234	98
					" 30	By Cotton,..........	2	86	75
					Aug. 5	By Insurance,.......	3	103	30
					Sep. 6	By do.	5	231	65
			656	68				656	68

Dr.			ROBERT MASON.				Cr.

1839					1839				
Aug. 15	To Bills Payable,....	3	3,625	00	July 30	By Cotton,..........	2	5,610	00
" 30	To Adven. to N. Orl.	3	2,600	00	Sep. 30	By Balance,.........	7	615	00
			6,225	00				6,225	00
	6,225 00								
	5,610 00								
	615 00								

7

Dr.			MURRAY		&	Co.			Cr.	
1839						1839				
July 31	To Bills Payable,....	2	2,400	00		Sep. 30	By Sales of Consign's,	6	5,314	50
Aug. 5	To Sundries,........	3	4,052	21		" "	By Balance,.........	7	1,137	71
			6,452	21					6,452	21

6,452 21
5,314 50
———
1,137 71

Dr.			CITY		BANK.				Cr.	
1839						1839				
July 3	To Cash,............	2	15,000	00		Sep. 14	By Cash,............	6	16,250	00
Aug.24	To do.	4	5,500	00		" 30	By Balance,.........	7	4,250	00
			20,500	00					20,500	00

20,500 00
16,250 00
———
4,250 00

Dr.			JOHN	STIRLING.					Cr.	
1839						1839				
Aug. 5	To Sundries,........	3	2,287	27		Aug. 1	By Bills Receivable, .	3	500	00
Sep. 30	To Balance,.........	7	2,695	63		Sep. 31	By Sales of Consign's,	6	4,482	90
			4,982	90					4,982	90

4,982 90
2,287 27
———
2,695 63

Dr.			EDWARD	ROBINSON.					Cr.	
1839						1839				
Aug.31	To Cotton,..........	4	1,705	20		Sep. 15	By Bills Receivable,.	5	1,000	00
			1,705	20		" 30	By Balance, ...	7	705	20
									1,705	20

1,705 20
1,000 00
———
705 20

8

Dr.			THOMAS JONES.			Cr.
1839			1839			
Aug. 31	To Cash,............ 4	150	00	Sep. 30	By Balance,......... 7	150	00

Dr.			JOHN REED.			Cr.
1839			1839			
Sep. 16	To Cash,............ 6	500	00	Sep. 30	By Balance,......... 7	500	00

Dr.			JAMES THOMPSON.			Cr.
1839			1839			
Sep. 12	To Bills Payable,.... 5	4,800	00	Sep. 1	By Merchandise,..... 5	12,000	00
" "	To Bills Receivable,. 5	2,500	00				
" 23	To Sales of Consign's, 6	2,622	50				
" 30	To Balance,......... 7	2,077	50				
		12,000	00			12,000	00

12,000 00
9,922 50

2,077 50

Dr.			VANDERPOOLE & CO.			Cr.
1839			1839			
Sep. 7	To Sundries,........ 5	3,785	43	Sep. 10	By Bills Receivable,. 5	2,500	00
				" 30	By Balance,......... 7	1,285	43
		3,785	43			3,785	43

3,785 43
2,500 00

1,285 43

9

Dr.				FENN & PARK.			Cr.	
1839				1839				
Sep. 13	To Sales of Consign's,	6	3,668	70	Sep. 27	By Bills Receivable, .	5	3,600	00
					" 28	By Cash,...........	6	68	70
			3,668	70				3,668	70

Dr.				THOMAS ATWOOD & CO.			Cr.	
1839				1839				
Sep. 25	To Sales of Consign's,	6	7,560	00	Sep. 30	By Balance,.........	7	7,560	00

Dr.				DAWSON & SONS.			Cr.	
1839				1839				
Sep. 26	To Sales of Consign's,	6	1,844	04	Sep. 30	By Balance, ...	7	1,844	04

Dr.				JAMES BROWN & CO.			Cr.	
1839				1839				
Sep. 28	To Sales of Consign's,	6	672	00	Sep. 30	By Balance,.........	7	672	00

Dr.				BALANCE.			Cr.	
1839				1839				
Sep. 30	To Sundries, ...	7	75,776	17	Sep. 30	By Sundries, ...	7	75,776	17

o

TRIAL BALANCE,

PROFIT AND LOSS AND BALANCE SHEETS.

SET II.

TRIAL BALANCE. — Set II.

	SEPTEMBER 30th, 1839.	— Drs. —		Totals.		— Crs. —		Totals.	
1	Stock,............................	12,500	00			62,500	00		
1	Profit and Loss,....................					241	40		
1	Commission,........................					1,050	37		
2	Ship Nero,.........................	10,900	00			3,300	00		
				23,400	00			67,091	77
2	Charges,...........................	1,669	32			668	74		
3	Cotton,............................	10,946	75			6,873	20		
3	Adventure to New Orleans,.........	2,093	00			2,600	00		
3	Adventure to Rotterdam,............	3,785	44						
				18,494	51			10,141	94
4	Cash,.............................	60,111	94			51,690	62		
4	Bills Receivable,..................	31,976	00			13,650	00		
4	Bills Payable,.....................	13,103	00			23,103	00		
5	Stephen Homer,....................	10,088	00			5,000	00		
				115,278	94			93,443	62
5	William Harris,...................	6,442	00			6,000	00		
5	James Forbes,.....................	3,226	00			3,026	00		
5	John Ramsay,......................	7,285	43			3,741	40		
6	W. Irving,.........................	2,300	00			5,228	40		
				19,253	43			17,995	80
6	Thomas Ryder,.....................					1,700	00		
6	Robert Mason,.....................	6,225	00			5,610	00		
7	Murray & Co.......................	6,452	21			5,314	50		
7	City Bank,.........................	20,500	00			16,250	00		
				33,177	21			28,874	50
7	John Stirling,.....................	2,287	27			4,982	90		
7	Edward Robinson,..................	1,705	20			1,000	00		
8	Thomas Jones,.....................	150	00						
8	John Reed,.........................	500	00						
				4,642	47			5,982	90
8	James Thompson,..................	9,922	50			12,000	00		
8	Vanderpoole & Co..................	3,785	43			2,500	00		
9	Thomas Atwood & Co..............	7,560	00						
9	Dawson & Sons,...................	1,844	04						
9	James Brown & Co.................	672	00						
				23,783	97			14,500	00
				238,030	53			238,030	53

Dr.	PROFIT AND LOSS SHEET.			Cr.		
To Charges,..................	1,000	58	By Commission,..............	1,050	37
Net gain,.....................	6,374	64	By Cotton,....................	1,176	45
			By ship Nero,................	4,400	00
			By Adventure to New Orleans,	507	00
			By Profit and Loss, ℘ Ledger,.	241	40
	7,375	22		7,375	22

Dr.	BALANCE SHEET.			*Cr.*	
— *Effects.* —			— *Debts.* —		
To ship Nero,	12,000	00	By Bills Payable,	10,000	00
To Cotton,	5,250	00	By William Irving,	2,928	40
To Adventure to Rotterdam,	3,785	44	By Thomas Ryder,	1,700	00
To Cash,	8,421	32	By John Stirling,	2,695	63
To Bills Receivable,	18,326	00	By James Thompson,	2,077	50
To Stephen Homer,	5,088	00	Amount of our Liabilities,	19,401	53
To William Harris,	442	00			
To James Forbes,	200	00	By Stock,.....*net capital,*	56,374	64
To John Ramsay,	3,544	03			
To Robert Mason,	615	00			
To Murray & Co.	1,137	71			
To City Bank,	4,250	00			
To Edward Robinson,	705	20			
To Thomas Jones,	150	00			
To John Reed,	500	00			
To Vanderpoole & Co.	1,285	43			
To Thomas Atwood & Co.	7,560	00			
To Dawson & Sons,	1,844	04			
To James Brown & Co.	672	00			
	75,776	17		75,776	17

BILL BOOK.—Set II.

Bills Receivable.

No.	When rec.d	On account of	On whom drawn.	Date.	Term.	When due.	Amount.	When and how disposed of.
	1839			1839		1839		1839
10	April 28	James Parker.	W. Morgan.	April 28	3 months.	July 31	5,000 00	July 31 In cash.
11	May 7	J. & W. Barker.	Thomas Nelson.	May 7	3 months.	Aug. 10	3,750 00	Aug. 10 In cash.
12	" 24	Thomas Wood.	Nevins & Co.	" 24	3 months.	" 27	1,250 00	" 27 In cash.
13	June 7	Stephen Homer.	Barclay & Co.	June 7	4 months.	Oct. 10	2,500 00	
14	" 23	Dawson & Sons.	Themselves.	" 23	4 months.	" 27	2,500 00	
							15,000 00	
15	July 12	Stephen Homer.	Holmes & Sons.	June 30	60 days' date.	Sept. 1	1,150 00	Sept. 1 In cash.
16	" 27	James Forbes.	James Benson & Son.	July 27	3 months.	Oct. 30	1,000 00	
							2,150 00	
17	Aug. 1	John Stirling.	Lloyd & Co.	Aug. 2	60 days' sight.	Oct. 4	500 00	
18	" 17	William Harris.	Sylvester & Co.	" 15	2 months.	" 18	2,500 00	
							3,000 00	
19	Sept. 10	Vanderpoole & Co.	Prime, Ward, & King.	Sept. 11	60 days' sight.	Nov. 13	2,500 00	Sept. 12 Ja.s Thompson.
20	" 15	E. Robinson.	Himself.	" 15	30 days' date.	Oct. 18	1,000 00	
21	" 20	W. Harris.	Jones & Co.	" 20	30 " "	" 23	3,000 00	
22	" 24	James Forbes.	Himself.	" 24	30 " "	" 27	1,726 00	
23	" 27	Fenn & Park.	Themselves.	" 20	30 " "	" 23	3,600 00	
							11,826 00	

Bills Payable.

No.	When accepted.	Drawn by	Payable to	Date.	Term.	When due.	Amount.	When and to whom paid.
	1839			1839		1839		1839
7	May 22	John Stirling.	Lloyd & Co.	May 18	2 months.	July 25	1,500 00	July 25 Merchants' Bank.
8	" 29	Thomas Cooper.	His order.	" 29	2 months.	Aug. 1	2,700 00	Aug. 1 "
9	June 7	Hope Insurance Co.	Thomas Wright.	June 7	3 months.	Sept. 10	800 00 / 5,000 00	Sept. 10 "
10	July 31	Murray & Co.	William Holmes.	July 20	60 days' sight.	Oct. 2	2,400 00	
11	" "	John Ramsay.	His order.	" 30	90 days' date.	Nov. 1	1,500 00 / 3,900 00	
12	Aug. 11	Crary & Co.	Their order.	Aug. 11	10 days' date.	Aug. 24	4,478 00	Aug. 24 Merchants' Bank.
13	" 15	R. Mason.	William Taylor.	" 15	30' " "	Sept. 17	3,625 00 / 8,103 00	Sept. 17 "
14	Sept. 8	William Irving.	Thomas Hill.	Sept. 8	3 months.	Dec. 11	1,300 00	
15	" 12	James Thompson.	His order.	" 12	4 months	1840 Jan. 15	4,800 00 / 6,100 00	

AN

IMPROVED JOURNAL,

COMBINING

SIMPLICITY AND ACCURACY.

EXPLANATORY REMARKS.

The transactions which compose the Introductory Set, are here Journalized upon an improved plan, which combines, in a great degree, the simplicity of Single with the advantages of Double Entry. This arrangement of the Journal is now followed by many extensive mercantile houses ; and perhaps no other form possessing equal facilities could be devised. It is applicable to any business where entries of the same kind occur frequently ; such as that of booksellers, retail dealers, jobbers, &c.

The improvements which have, from time to time, been effected in book-keeping, do not comprehend any change in the *principles* of Double Entry, but only in the form and arrangement of the books.

EXPLANATION. — This Journal is ruled with three money columns on the *Dr.* side, and three similar columns on the *Cr.* side, between which the transactions are entered in the usual technical form. The 'Cash' and 'Merchandise' columns exhibit the amount of cash received and paid, and of goods bought and sold. These amounts are carried to the Ledger only once a month, which saves time, and prevents the merchandise and cash accounts from extending to a great length, which, by posting each entry *singly*, is unavoidable. The personal accounts, and all other entries except cash and merchandise, are to be arranged in the columns headed 'Sundries,' the *Drs.* in the left, and the *Crs.* in the right hand column : these are to be posted daily, in the usual manner. By adding the columns headed 'Merchandise,' 'Cash,' and 'Sundries,' the accuracy of the Journal is ascertained ; for, if correct, the aggregate of the *Drs.* must be equal to that of the *Crs.* In this specimen the 'Cash' is Journalized daily ; but it might, with equal propriety, be entered weekly or monthly.

166

Mdze.	Cash.	Sundries.	— Drs. — NEW YORK, January 1, 1839. — Crs. —	Sundries.	Cash.	Mdze.
	15,000 00	....	CASH Dr. to Stock, Capital in trade,................	15,000 00		
			——— 2 ———			
		325 38	CHARGES Dr. to Cash, Paid for Stationery, &c.........	....	325 38	
			——— 4 ———			
8,151 25	....	....	MERCHANDISE Dr. to C. Hammond, Goods, as ℔ Invoice,...........	8,151 25		
			——— 6 ———			
		957 12	J. BRUCE & CO. Dr. to Merchandise, 15 pieces Broadcloth, ℔ B. P....	....	....	957 12
			——— 7 ———			
2,125 75	....	....	MERCHANDISE Dr. to Cash, Goods purchased, as ℔ B. P....	....	2,125 75	
			——— 9 ———			
857 75	....	....	MERCHANDISE Dr. to Bills Payable, My Acceptance favor Houe & Co. at 30 days,...................	857 75		
			——— 12 ———			
		25 18	CHARGES Dr. to Cash, Paid for Advertising, Postage, &c.	....	25 18	
			——— 15 ———			
		785 50	BILLS RECEIVABLE Dr. to Mdze. J. Hill's Note, at 90 days,.......	....	....	785 50
			——— 18 ———			
	280 31	....	CASH Dr. to Merchandise, For sales this day,............	....	....	280 31
			——— 19 ———			
		4,000 00	C. HAMMOND Dr. to Bills Payable, Accepted his Draft, at 90 days,..	4,000 00		
			——— 25 ———			
		957 12	BILLS REC'LE Dr. to J. Bruce & Co. My Draft on them, at 10 days' sight, ...	957 12		
			——— 28 ———			
		600 00	SUNDRIES Dr. to Merchandise, Goods sold to J. Brown & Son,...	....	....	1,200 00
	600 00	....	Bills Rec'le, their Note at 90 days, Cash........for balance,........			
			——— 29 ———			
		4,151 25	CHARLES HAMMOND Dr. to Cash, For balance of account,........	....	4,151 25	
			——— 30 ———			
		989 75	JAMES BRUCE & CO. Dr. to Mdze. Goods amounting to.....;.......	....	....	989 75
11,134 75	15,880 31	12,791 30	.........Carried forward,........	26,956 12	6,627 56	4,212 68

Ledger folio.

Mdze.	Cash.	Sundries.	— *Drs.* — NEW YORK, *January* 31, 1839. — *Crs.* —	Sundries.	Cash.	Mdze.
11,134 75	15,880 31	12,791 30	........Brought forward,........	28,966 12	6,627 56	4,212 68
		15 78	CHARGES *Dr. to Cash*, Paid Postages, &c..............	....	15 78	
			Monthly Totals.			
11,134 75	15,880 31	12,807 08	..........Sundries, ...	28,966 12	6,643 34	4,212 68
		15,880 31	...........Cash,.................	6,643 34		
		11,134 75	.........Merchandise,..........	4,212 68		
		39,822 14	..........Total,...................	39,822 14		
			— FEBRUARY 1, 1839. —			
583 40	....	....	MERCHANDISE *Dr. to C. Hammond*, Goods, ℔ B. of P..............	583 40		
			4			
		350 22	SUNDRIES *Dr. to Merchandise*, For sales this day,............. James Peters, Goods amounting to	....	....	1,755 85
		575 88	Rufus Dean, // //			
		829 75	Henry Pope, // //			
			6			
	957 12	....	CASH *Dr. to Bills Receivable*, Received am't of Bruce & Co.'s Acceptance,...................	957 12		
			8			
		1,755 85	BILLS RECEIVABLE *Dr. to Sundries*, Rec'd the following Bills this day :			
			To J. Peters, from 4th, at 30 days,	350 22		
			To R. Dean, // // //	575 88		
			To H. Pope, // // //	829 75		
			10			
517 97	....	....	MERCHANDISE *Dr. to Sundries*, As ℔ purchases this day,.......			
			To Charles Hammond, ℔ Invoice,	387 97		
			To Buchanan & Co. //	78 25		
			To James Finlay & Co. //	51 75		
			//			
		8 25	CHARGES *Dr. to Cash*, For Postage, &c........... ..	....	8 25	
			//			
			SUNDRIES *Dr. to Bills Receivable*, For Pope's Note, discounted at the Bank of Commerce,.......	829 75		
	826 20	....	Cash received,..................			
		3 55	Profit and Loss, discount charged by Bank,..................			
			//			
		785 50	C. HAMMOND *Dr. to Bills Rec'ble*, Endorsed Hill's Note to his order,	785 50		
			//			
		857 75	BILLS PAYABLE *Dr. to Cash*, Paid Acceptance favor Hone & Co.	....	857 75	
1,101 37	1,783 32	5,166 75	........Carried forward,........	5,429 59	866 00	1,755 85

Ledger folio.

Mdze.	Cash.	Sundries.	— Drs. — NEW YORK, *February* 10, 1839. — Crs. —	Sundries.	Cash.	Mdze.
1,101 37	1,783 32	5,166 75	........Brought forward,........	5,429 59	866 00	1,755 85
1,800 00	....	....	MERCHANDISE *Dr. to Sundries*, Invoice of Goods purchased of Simpson & Co................ To B. Payable, my Note at 60 days, To Cash.......for balance,.......	1,000 00	800 00	
			———— 28 ————			
		1,579 23	JAMES BRUCE & Co. *Dr. to Mdze.* Goods ⅌ B. P.................	....	....	1,579 23
			"			
		58 97	CHARGES *Dr. to Cash*, Paid on Shipment, &c...........	....	58 97	
2,901 37	1,783 32	6,804 95 1,783 32 2,901 37	*Monthly Totals.* ....Sundries, ...Cash,................. ....Merchandise, ...	6,429 59 1,724 97 3,335 08	1,724 97	3,335 08
		11,489 64	..........Total,.................	11,489 64		
			———— MARCH 1, 1839. ————			
		27 14	INSURANCE *Dr. to Bills Payable*, My Note to Globe Insurance Co.	27 14		
			"			
		1,039 92	J. DANA & Co. *Dr. to Sundries*, For Invoice ⅌ Jane, To Merchandise, Goods am'tng to To Charges......at shipping,.... To Insurance....as above,....... To Commission..on Insurance,..	.... 31 42 27 14 5 52	....	975 84
			———— 2 ————			
		93 48	GEORGE SMITH *Dr. to Sundries*, For Insurance on Cons't ⅌ Ann, To Cash paid Premium and Policy, To Commission,.................	.... 16 20	77 28	
			———— 3 ————			
		989 75	BILLS REC'LE *Dr. to J. Bruce & Co.* Their Acceptance at 30 days,....	989 75		
			———— 4 ————			
		220 27	CHARGES *Dr. to Cash*, On Produce ⅌ Ann,...........	....	220 27	
			———— 5 ————			
		896 75	JAMES PETERS *Dr. to Smith's Sales*, For 20 bales Cotton ⅌ Ann,....	896 75		
			———— 7 ————			
		78 25	BUCHANAN & Co. *Dr. to Cash*, Balance of account, ...	....	78 25	
			———— 8 ————			
		31 58	PROFIT & LOSS *Dr. to J. Bruce & Co.* Discount allowed, ...	31 58		
		3,377 14	.........Carried forward,........	2,025 50	375 80	975 84

(Ledger folio.)

— Drs. —			NEW YORK, *March* 12, 1839.		— Crs. —	
Mdze.	Cash.	Sundries.		Sundries.	Cash.	Mdze.
		3,377 14	........*Brought forward,*........	2,025 50	372 80	975 84
		896 75	SMITH's SALES *Dr. to Sundries,* As ⅌ Account-Sales rendered of Cotton ⅌ Ann,............. To Charges,......for freight, &c.. To Commission,..mine on sales,.. To George Smith,..for net proceeds,	85 30 35 87 775 58		
			———— 15 ————			
		1,039 92	BILLS REC'LE *Dr. to J. Dunn & Co.* Their Acceptance at 90 days,....	1,039 92		
			———— 17 ————			
		61 34	INSURANCE *Dr. to Cash,* Prem. & Policy on Goods ⅌ Nero,	....	61 34	
			———— 18 ————			
		85 39	CHARGES *Dr. to Cash,* Various expenses on shipments,	....	85 39	
			———— 19 ————			
		2,759 88	GEORGE SMITH *Dr. to Sundries,* Invoice ⅌ Nero,............. To Merchandise,..amounting to.. To Charges ....at shipping,...... To Insurance, for Prem. & Policy, To Commission,................	.... 75 37 61 34 72 87	....	2,550 30
			———— 21 ————			
		3,360 25	BUCHANAN &Co. *Dr. to Smith's S's.* 15 hhds. Sugar ⅌ Ann,..........	3,360 25		
			———— 25 ————			
		27 14	BILLS PAYABLE *Dr. to Cash,* Paid Note favor Globe Ins. Co...	....	27 14	
			———— " ————			
		51 75	J. FINLAY & Co. *Dr. to Cash,* Paid them in full,..............	....	51 75	
			———— " ————			
		45 78	CHARGES *Dr. to Cash,* Paid expenses on Produce ⅌ Ann,	....	45 78	
			———— " ————			
		3,360 25	SMITH's SALES *Dr. to Sundries,* ⅌ Acc. Sales ren'd Sugar ⅌ Ann, To Charges,........freight, &c... To Commission ....on sales,..... To George Smith,..net proceeds,.	180 75 134 41 3,045 09		
			———— 31 ————			
		450 00	CHARGES *Dr. to Cash,* Rent and Clerk's Salary.,.......	....	450 00	
		15,515 59	*Monthly Totals.* ....Sundries, ...Cash,............... ....Merchandise,..........	10 892 25 1,097 20 3,526 14	1,097 20	3,526 14
		15,515 59	..........Total,................	15,515 59		

Mem. — The merchandise in store amounts to $5,786 00.

EXPLANATION

OF

COMMERCIAL TERMS OR EXPRESSIONS

ABANDONMENT. Its most ordinary application in commercial transactions is to marine insurances : it then signifies the exercise of a right, which the *assured* claims, to call upon underwriters or insurers to accept of what is saved, and to pay the full amount of the insurance, as if a total loss had happened.

ABATEMENT. A discount allowed for prompt payment : it is likewise allowed at the custom-house on goods which have received damage by salt water, &c.

ACCEPTANCE. An engagement to pay a bill, when due, according to the tenor of the acceptance.

ACCOMMODATION, when applied to bills or notes, are those for which no value has been given; that is, when the drawee only lends his name; and that the drawer engages to provide him with the means of payment when the bill falls due.

ACCOUNT-CURRENT. A statement of mercantile transactions with correspondents, drawn out in a plain and circumstantial manner, in the form of *Dr.* and *Cr.*, showing how affairs stood between the parties at the time when the account was made up.

ACCOUNT-SALES. An account of goods sold on commission, drawn out by the agent to whom they were consigned, to be sent to his employer, or the person who made the consignment.

ADMINISTRATOR. A person to whom the court commits the administration of the goods of a person deceased, in default of an executor.

ADVANCE. Money paid before goods are delivered, or, in case of consignment, before they are sold.

ADVENTURE. When a merchant exports goods to or from a foreign market, on his own account and risk, it is called an individual speculation, or adventure, to or from that place.

ADVICE. Mercantile intelligence. To *advise a bill* is to describe the amount, date, term, to whom payable, &c.. and request the person on whom drawn to accept it.

AGENT. A person duly empowered to do business for another. The duty of an agent is to procure the best intelligence of the state of trade at the place where he resides — of the quantity and quality of the goods in the market — their present prices, and the probability of their rising or falling — to pay exact obedience to the orders of employers — to consult their interest in all matters referred to his discretion — to execute their business with all the despatch which circumstances will admit — and to be distinct and correct in his accounts.

ANNUITY. A periodical payment of money, either yearly, half-yearly, quarterly, weekly, or at any other intervals.

ANNUL, in book-keeping, signifies to render an article of no import in the account. Instead of *erasing a sum* which has been entered by mistake on the *Cr.* side of an account, the account is *debited* for the same sum ; and, on the contrary, if a sum has been entered on the *Dr.* side, the same sum is placed to the *Cr.* side of the account.

ARBITRATION. The determination of a cause by persons mutually chosen by the parties.

ASSIGNEE. A person deputed by another to manage the affairs of a bankrupt.

ATTACHMENT. The act by which a creditor may claim and seize the effects of his debtor, wherever they may be found.

AVERAGE. A contribution made for losses at sea. Averages are distinguished into *general* and *particular*. *General Average* is a proportionable contribution paid by all the proprietors of a ship and cargo for losses which are made with a view to safety, such as throwing goods overboard, or cutting away masts to prevent shipwreck. *Particular Average* is a contribution for such damages or losses as may happen from the common accidents of sea.

AWARD. The judgment of arbitration of one or more persons, at the request of two parties who are at variance, for ending the matter in dispute.

BALANCE OF TRADE. The difference between the commercial exports and imports of one country with respect to another.

BALANCE. The difference between the *Dr.* and *Cr.* sides of an account in a merchant's books.

BANKS. BANKING-HOUSES. Establishments wherein the various operations of banking are carried on. The former term is more properly applied to such as belong to Joint Stock Companies trading under an assumed title, whose capital is subscribed by a numerous body of shareholders, and whose affairs are managed by a cashier and a board of directors ; the latter, to a few individuals in copartnership, trading on their own capital and in their own names. The system of banking affords many advantages and facilities for business, the principal of which are the following. It provides places of safety for the custody of money. It obviates the inconvenience of carrying cash from place to place at the risk of loss or robbery. It effects a great saving of time, and consequently of expense, to merchants and tradesmen, who would otherwise have to count out every sum of money they have to pay, and to send their own clerks to all parts of the town to demand payment of their notes and drafts. The term *bank* is derived from *banco*, the Italian word for *bench*, as the Lombard Jews in Italy kept *benches* in the market-place, where they exchanged money and bills. When a banker failed, his bench was broken by the populace ; and from this circumstance we have the term *bankrupt.*

BANKRUPT. A trader whom misfortune or extravagance has rendered unable to pay his debts.

BARTER. The exchanging of one commodity for another : such was the original mode of commerce till money was invented.

BILL. A term generally applied to a draft or promissory note, and frequently to an account of goods.

BILL OF ENTRY. A list of the particulars of goods entered at the custom-house.

BILL OF LADING. A printed agreement between the shipper of goods and the captain of a ship, binding the latter to deliver them, "in good order and well conditioned," on payment of a certain freight. It is usual to make out three bills, one to the shipper, the second to be held by the captain, and the third to be sent to the person to whom the goods are consigned, by which he can claim them on their arrival.

BILL OF SALE. A contract, under seal, whereby a person conveys the right and interest which he has in goods and chattels.

BILL OF STORE. A license granted by the custom-house to merchants, to carry such stores and provisions as are necessary for a voyage, free of duty.

BILL OF EXCHANGE. A written order for the payment of money, issued from one place, and directed to another.

BLANK CREDIT. The permission which one house gives to another to draw on it to a certain extent, at any time, for their own accommodation.

BOUNTY. A premium given for the encouragement of some branch of trade, manufacture, or agriculture.

BONDED GOODS. Certain articles, which, on being landed, are warehoused, upon bond being given by the owner for the payment of duties, &c.

BOTTOMRY. A contract in the nature of a mortgage of a ship, when the owner of it borrows money to enable him to carry on a voyage, and pledges the keel or *bottom* of the ship as a security for the repayment; and it is understood that, if the vessel be lost, the lender loses his money.

BROKER. An agent employed by merchants in buying and selling, who, for a trifling charge, finds the merchant buyers in one case, and sellers in the other. There are several kinds of brokers — such as ship brokers, insurance brokers, exchange brokers, stock brokers, &c.

BROKERAGE. A commission or per centage paid by merchants to brokers, either for the sale or purchase of goods, bills of exchange, stock, &c.

CASE OF NEED, ACCEPTANCE, AND PAYMENT FOR HONOR. Every individual, whose name is found upon a bill, whether as drawer, drawee, or endorser, is alike responsible to the last holder for its payment when due ; and, as the return of a bill is not only prejudicial to the credit of a merchant, but is also attended with considerable expense, a plan has been devised for guarding against this unpleasant occurrence. This plan consists in adding what is called "*A Case of Need*," or reference to a correspondent in the same place, who is thus called upon "*to interfere for honor*" of the merchant by whom the bill is referred to him. This reference is made by writing at the bottom of the bill, thus: — "In case of need, with Messrs. ———." When acceptance or payment is refused by the drawee, the holder applies to the house thus indicated, who accept or pay, as the case may be, *under Protest and Act of Honor;* such being the name given to the notarial instrument drawn up to enable their correspondent for whose account they interfere, to recover from the drawers of the bill.

CAPITAL, or STOCK. The effects of a house in money or wares, by means of which it carries on trade and supports its credit.

CHARTER PARTY. The engagement between the owner of a ship and the merchant, who engages the whole ship to go from one port to another with goods, for a certain sum.

CHECK; sometimes called a DRAFT. An order addressed to a bank for the payment of money to the individual named, or bearer, on demand. Checks are negotiable, like bills, but require no endorsement, and are payable instantly on presentation. All checks should be presented for payment with as little delay as possible; for, if retained beyond the day of their dates, and the banks on whom they are drawn should fail, the holder cannot recover from the drawer. On opening an account with a bank, every person is required to write his name in a book, in order that his signature may be known and always referred to when necessary. He is then supplied with a cash-book and printed checks. In the former, all the sums received and paid on his account are entered to his debit and credit, as frequently as he chooses to leave the book for that purpose. When he has an occasion to pay an account, or to draw cash for his own use, he has only to fill up and sign a check, and the bank immediately pays it.

CHEVISANCE. A composition between debtor and creditor.

CIRCULATING MEDIUM. Cash, bank notes, or other paper money payable on demand.

CIRCULAR LETTER. The printed notice of the establishment or dissolution of a house, or alteration in the firm, &c. See FIRM.

CLEARING. The name given to a daily exchange of bills and checks, which takes place between most of the bankers resident in the city of London, at the clearing-house in Lombard Street. The banking-houses who "*clear*" are thirty in number, and a clerk from each attends, first at twelve, and then at three o'clock, with all the bills and drafts on the others that have been paid in up to those hours. There is a drawer appropriated to each house, and in these all the drafts and bills are distributed by the respective clerks. Each being provided with a printed list of the clearing bankers, called a *balance sheet,* he enters to the debit side all the sums the other houses owe him, and on the credit all that he owes them. If he has money to receive, he takes it from any body who has money to pay; for it is obvious that the amount to be paid must be equal to the amount to be received; and the only point to be attended to is, that each shall obtain the balance due to him on the clearing.

CLEARING A VESSEL, is entering all particulars relating to her at the custom-house.

COMMISSION. An allowance given to agents or factors for transacting the business of others, always so much per cent.

COMPROMISE. To adjust a dispute by mutual concessions.

COMPOSITION. A contract between an insolvent debtor and his creditors, by which the latter accept of a *part of the debt,* in compensation for the whole.

CONSIGNMENT. Goods sent by one house to another to sell for their account, allowing them so much per cent for their trouble. See COMMISSION.

CONSUL. An accredited agent of government at a foreign port, appointed to protect the maritime interests of the country more especially. Documents of any kind, attested by the consul under his hand and seal of office, are admitted as evidence in courts of justice.

CONTRABAND TRADE. That which is prohibited by law.

CONTINGENT. The proportion that falls to the share of a person concerned in any business or advantage.

CONVOY. Ships of war sailing with other ships in order to protect them.

COUNTER-ORDER. An order sent to revoke a former one, either for the sale or purchase of any commodity.

CREDIT. In general, the confidence which one house reposes in another; more particularly, the reverse of DEBIT.

CURRENCY. The money in circulation, as distinguished from bank paper, &c.

CURRENT. A term used to express the present time. Hence, the *price current* of any merchandise is the known or ordinary price at the time it is published.

P *

CUSTOM-HOUSE. The place where entries are made on goods exported or imported, and the duties imposed by law paid.

DAYS OF GRACE. A customary number of days allowed for the payment of a bill after the same becomes due.

DEMAND. Calling upon a man for any sum of money, or any other thing due. A bill at sight, therefore, is payable on demand.

DEBENTURE. A certificate given by the proper officers of the customs on certain goods exported, on which the exporter or seller is entitled to a drawback or bounty.

DEL CREDERE. A per centage made by merchants in selling goods, for guaranteeing the solidity of the purchaser.

DEMURRAGE. A penalty incurred by merchants for delaying a ship beyond the time specified in her charter party.

DEVIATION. A departure without legal cause from the regular course of a voyage, which deviation incapacitates the insured from recovering, in case of loss.

DISHONOR. An expression made use of when bills of exchange, &c., are refused acceptance or payment.

DIVIDEND. A share of any capital, debt, or profit; also the interest in the stocks.

DOCK. A place where vessels are built, repaired, laid up, or lodged for loading or unloading.

DRAFT. A bill or check by which one person draws money on another; also, a small allowance on goods sold by weight.

DRAWEE. The person on whom bills of exchange are drawn.

DRAWBACK. A premium allowed on exportations.

DUE PROTECTION. Regular acceptance or payment of a draft or bill.

DUBIOUS PAPER. Bills drawn on houses of little credit.

DUTY. Tax imposed by government upon the import or export of goods.

EFFECTS. Moneys, goods, or movables, in the hands of one person, belonging to another.

EMBARGO. An arrest on ships or merchandise by public authority.

EMPORIUM. A principal place for the importation and sale of merchandise.

ENDORSEMENT. The signature which the holder of a negotiable bill writes on the back of it, by which he transfers his interest to a third person.

EXCHANGE. A place in most large cities, where merchants, agents, bankers, brokers, and other commercial characters, meet, to confer and treat together of matters relating to exchanges, remittances, payments, adventures, freights, assurance, and other mercantile negotiations, both by sea and land.

EXCHANGES. The paying or receiving of money in one country for its equivalent in the money of another country, by means of bills of exchange.

FAILURE. Where a person in trade, through misfortune or imprudence, is unable to pay his debts.

FINANCES. A term generally applied to the public revenues.

FIRM. The mercantile appellation of a house engaged in commerce.

FIRSTS FOR ACCEPTANCE. When a merchant purchases a foreign bill, (for the *first, second,* and *third* constitute but one bill,) he transmits the first immediately to a correspondent in or near the town on which it is drawn, to procure acceptance to it. By this means he secures the responsibility of the drawee, without delay, and without incurring any risk whatever, since the first, not being endorsed, is not negotiable; and in the mean time he can dispose of the second, writing it at foot, " First, with Messrs. ———.' The second, travelling, as it must ultimately do, to the place on which it is drawn, is presented to the house indicated in the above notice; and the first is immediately given up, being, in the language of merchants, *held at the disposal of the second.*

FIRST-RATE PAPER. Bills drawn or accepted by a good house, such as has always paid its bills regularly.

FLAT. An article of merchandise is said to be *flat* when there are few buyers.

FORESTALLING. The purchasing and laying up goods before they come to market, with the intention of raising the price.

FOLIO. The debtor and creditor side of a ledger or account-book.

FREIGHT. The sum paid for transporting merchandise by sea, &c.

GOVERNMENT. "For your government," is an expression adopted from the French, signifying, " in order to give you better information, and rules for acting by, in the purchase or sale of any merchandise."

GUARANTEE. A person who undertakes that certain stipulations shall be fulfilled.

HONOR. *To honor a draft* is to accept it on presentation.

IMPORTATION. The act of bringing goods into a country from foreign parts

INDEMNITY. Where one person secures another from responsibility against any particular event.

INSOLVENT. A person in trade who

has not a capital adequate to the payment of his debts.

INSTALMENTS. Certain proportions, in which, by agreement between debtor and creditor, a sum due is to be paid, at stipulated times.

INSURANCE, or ASSURANCE. A contract of indemnity, by which one party engages, for a stipulated sum, to insure another against a risk to which he is exposed. The party who takes upon him the risk is called the *Insurer*, or *Underwriter;* and the party protected by the insurance is called the *Insured;* the sum paid is called the *Premium;* and the instrument containing the contract is called the *Policy.*

INSURANCE BROKER. A person employed by merchants to effect insurance on their ships and cargoes.

INTEREST. A premium paid for the use or loan of money. To guard a person's *interest* is to protect his property, and watch over his concerns.

INVENTORY. An account or catalogue of effects ; a schedule.

INVOICE. A paper sent off with goods exported on commission, or for the shipper's own account.

JOURNAL. A book, in which is recorded the transactions of the *Day Book*, and the subsidiary ones, having the *Drs.* and *Crs.* pointed out, in order to post them with more ease into the Ledger.

LAND-WAITER. An officer belonging to the custom-house, whose duty it is to take an account of goods imported.

LEASE. A contract, by which, in consideration of some payment, a temporary possession is granted of houses or lands.

LEDGER. The principal book of accounts kept by merchants and tradesmen, in which the state of every person's account is seen.

LETTER OF ADVICE. A letter giving notice of any transaction.

LETTER OF ATTORNEY, or POWER OF ATTORNEY. A writing which empowers one person therein named to act for another.

LETTER OF CREDIT. A letter by which one person can receive money on the credit of another.

LETTER OF LICENSE. A written permission, granted to a person under embarrassment, allowing him to conduct his affairs for a certain time without molestation.

LICENSE. A privilege from government for carrying on a trade or business on which a certain duty is laid.

LIEN. A claim, or attachment, on any property which a person has in his possession, for a debt due to him from the owner of the property.

LIGHTERAGE. A charge for carrying goods to and from a ship, in a lighter.

LIQUIDATION. The winding up of a business, such as paying and receiving all debts, &c.

MANIFEST. A list of a ship's cargo, which paper must be signed by the master of the vessel, before any of the goods can be landed.

MANUFACTURE. An article produced by labor or machinery from any raw material.

MANUFACTORY. A place where several artificers are making any commodity or article of merchandise.

MART. A place of public traffic ; a great market or fair.

MATURITY IN BILLS is when they become due or payable.

MAXIMUM. The highest price of any article, as fixed by some law or regulation.

MERCHANDISE. All sorts of goods which may be bought or sold.

MERCHANT. A wholesale dealer in all sorts of goods on his own account.

MINIMUM. The lowest price of any article, as fixed by some regulation.

MINT. The place where the public or current money is coined.

MONOPOLY. The sole power or privilege of selling any commodity, whereby any person, or bodies politic or corporate, are sought to be restrained of any freedom they had before.

MUTUAL DEBTS. When two traders are indebted to each other, one debt may be set off against the other ; and, in case of bankruptcy, mutual credits, as well as mutual debts, may be set off.

MUTUAL PROMISE. When one person promises to another to pay money, or do some other act, and he, in consideration thereof, promises to do a certain act, &c.

NATIONAL DEBT. A debt due by any whole political community, as represented by their legislature and government.

NET PROCEEDS. The sum which goods produce after every deduction is made.

NET WEIGHT. The weight of any commodity, after every deduction is made, and for which the price is charged.

NON CLAIM. Where a creditor neglects to make his claim within a proper time, in which case he cannot enforce his demand.

NOTARY PUBLIC. A person duly appointed to attest deeds and writings : he also notes or protests bills of exchange, inland and foreign, and promissory notes, when refused or returned.

NOTING. The act of a notary when a

bill or draft is not duly honored, or, in other words, refused acceptance or payment.

OBLIGATION. A bond containing a penalty, with a condition annexed either for the payment of money, performance of covenants, or the like.

OFFICE. A place where business is transacted.

OMNIUM. A term used among stock-jobbers to express all the articles included in the contracts between government and the original subscribers to a loan.

ORDER. A direction from one house to another to effect certain purchases, &c., upon limited or unlimited conditions.

PACKAGE. Any quantity of goods tied up for carriage. The latter term also denotes the charge made for tying up the goods.

PAR OF EXCHANGE. The intrinsic value of the money of one country compared with that of another, with respect both to the weight and fineness.

PARCEL. A term applied both to small packages of wares and to large lots of goods. In this last sense, 20 hhds. of sugar or more, if bought at one price, or in a single lot, are denominated "a parcel of sugar."

PARTNERSHIP. When two or more persons unite in trade, and agree to participate in the profits or losses, according to their respective shares in the capital employed in the concern.

PART OWNERS. Persons concerned in ship matters, and who have joint shares therein.

PASS IN CONFORMITY. To acknowledge that an account transmitted is correct.

PLEASE DO THE NEEDFUL. A technical phrase used by merchants in their correspondence, which means, "Do all that is requisite in the case."

PIERAGE. Money paid for the support of an established pier.

POLICY OF ASSURANCE. The deed or instrument by which a contract of assurance is effected.

PORTAGE. Money paid for sailors' wages while in port; also, money paid for the use of a port in shipping or landing goods.

POSTING, in book-keeping, is the mode of transferring articles from the Journal or the Subsidiary Books to the Ledger.

PREMIUM. The money paid an underwriter for insuring the safety of ships, goods, houses, &c.

PRICE CURRENT. A list of the various articles of merchandise in the market, with the present prices annexed to each. In most of the great commercial cities and towns, lists of this description are generally published once or twice a week.

PRINCIPAL. The capital sum due or lent, in opposition to interest. It also means the head of a *firm* or commercial house.

PRO FORMA. Imaginary, fictitious. The utility of a *pro forma* document is this :— A Hamburg merchant is desirous of shipping a parcel of wools to London on speculation, and, in order to ascertain whether he can realize a profit by such a consignment, applies to his correspondent for a *pro forma* account-sales of wool. The merchant in London either transmits him a copy of a real account, suppressing names, marks, &c., or makes up one altogether fictitious, but which suffices to show the duties, charges, commission, and expenses of all kinds, on wools in the port of London.

PROMISSORY NOTE. A note of hand purporting the payment of a certain sum at a stated period.

PROTEST. A paper made out by a notary public, declaring a bill has been presented for acceptance or payment, and was refused.

PRIMAGE. So much per cent generally allowed to the captain of a ship on the amount of freight.

PROCURATION. The power of using the signature of a house on letters and bills.

QUARANTINE. The time a ship suspected of infection is restricted from intercourse with the shore; also, certain duties imposed on ships.

QUOTED ON BOARD. The price for which a merchant agrees to put goods on board free of expenses of shipping to the buyer.

REBATE. An allowance, in the purchase of goods, for prompt payment.

RECEIPT. An acknowledgment in writing of having received a sum of money or other value, and is either a voucher for an obligation discharged or one incurred.

RESPONDENTIA. A contract by which money is borrowed on the security of goods and merchandise, the same as in bottomry on the security of a ship.

RESTITUTION. When money has been paid wrongfully or by mistake, the person so paying has a right to demand it back.

RETIRE. In mercantile phraseology, to *retire a bill* means, to pay it, or to take it out of circulation by some other means.

RETAIL. A dealing in commodities in small quantities.

RETURNS. A term expressing the

value, in goods or in money, returned by the consignee of a cargo or parcel of goods to the consigner. The term also means, a return or remittance of bills.

RETURN OF PREMIUM. The whole or part of the premium of an insurance which is given back in terms of the *policy.*

REMITTANCE. A sum of money sent, either in bills of exchange or otherwise, from one house to another.

RENEWAL OF A BILL. The cancelling of a bill or promissory note due, and accepting another, at a given date, in lieu thereof.

SAMPLE. A small quantity of an article, at a public or private sale, as a specimen of the commodity.

SALVAGE. A certain allowance due to those through whose instrumentality property is saved from the perils of the seas, enemies, &c.

SCHEDULE. The statement of a bankrupt's affairs delivered by him to the commissioners appointed to investigate his case.

SEARCHER. An officer of the customhouse, whose business is to search all ships outward bound, to see whether any prohibited or uncustomed goods are on board.

SEA-WORTHY. When a ship is, in every respect, fitted for her destined voyage.

SEIZURE. An arrest of some merchandise, movable or other matter, either in consequence of some law or express order of the government.

SET-OFF OF MUTUAL DEBTS. Where tradesmen are mutually indebted, one debt may be set against the other ; and, in case any action be brought, notice is to be given of the particular sum or debt intended to be *set off* against another.

SMUGGLING. The act of importing or exporting goods without payment of the customs or excise duties.

SOLIDITY. The character which a mercantile house bears as to property.

STAPLE GOODS. Such as are sold at a staple ; or, the principal produce of a country ; and also goods not being liable to perish, as wood, lead, iron, &c.

STOCK. A fund raised by a commercial company to be employed in trade : in book-keeping, it denotes the owner or owners of the books. *Stocks* is a term likewise applied to the capitals of banks.

SURETY. When one person becomes bound that another shall pay a certain debt or perform a certain act.

TALLY. A cleft piece of wood to score any account or reckoning upon.

TARE. An allowance for the weight of the bag, box, cask, or other package in which the goods are packed up.

TARIFF. A table or catalogue containing the names of different kinds of merchandise, with the duties to be paid.

TELLERS. Clerks in banks and public offices, who reckon, receive, and pay money.

TIDEWAITERS. Officers employed to see the loading and unloading of ships, in order to prevent contraband trade.

TONNAGE. The admeasurement of a ship, by which she pays the tonnage duty ; or, it is her actual capacity for stowage, and is, in that case, not unfrequently called her *burthen.*

TRUSTEE. A person who has an estate or money put or trusted in his hands for the use of another.

UMPIRE. When two arbitrators cannot agree in settling a dispute, a third person is named, who is called an *umpire,* and whose decision is binding.

UNDERWRITERS. Persons who insure ships, cargoes, or other risks; which is performed by writing their names under a policy of insurance.

USURY consists in taking more than legal interest for the loan of money.

VALUE. *To value,* in a mercantile sense, is to draw a bill. The words " value received," or " value in account," are always mentioned in every bill of exchange.

WHARFAGE. Money paid for the use of a wharf.

23

EQUATION OF PAYMENTS,

OR

AVERAGE TIMES OF PAYMENTS

To find the average time at which several sums of money, due at different periods, may be paid, so that no loss shall be sustained by either the debtor or creditor, is called *Equating*, or reducing the times of payment to one. For example : —

A. owes B. $440, whereof $200 is payable in 2 years, $160 is payable in 3½ years, and the balance, $80, is payable in 4½ years. Now, at what period may B. receive the whole amount, so that the interest accruing on the sums which are overdue, may be counterbalanced by the discount on the sums which are not yet due ?

The sum due at the end of the first period, if not paid till the last period, will have the interest accruing on it during the intermediate time. The sum due at the second period, if not paid till the last, will likewise have the interest accruing upon it during the interval between the second and last period ; and so on. Now, these several interests added together, will give the whole interest, if all the money were to be paid at the last period. But this would not fulfil the intended purpose, which is to discover a precise intermediate time, at which the interest due upon the portions payable before that time, would amount to the same sum as the discount receivable upon the portions payable after that time. By calculating interest upon the different portions, from the various periods of payment up to the day when the last sum is due, we have found what amount of principal and interest would be due if the whole debt were to be discharged at that period. To fulfil the intended purpose, and annul the interest, we must ascertain what number of days' interest upon the entire principal will equal the aggregate interest upon the individual sums; and, anticipating by that number of days the time at which the last payment will be due, we ascertain precisely the period at which the interest due upon the portions forborne is equal to the discount receivable upon the portions anticipated; in other words, we have discovered the equation of payment. For this purpose men of business use the following general

RULE.

Multiply the amount of each debt by the time it has to run till it becomes due, and divide the sum of the products by the amount of the debt; the quotient is the average or equated time of payment.

Thus the equated time of payment in the preceding example is ascertained as follows: —

Amounts.		*Years.*			
200	multiplied by	2	. . .	equals 400	
160	"	$3\frac{1}{2}$	. . .	" 560	
80	"	$4\frac{1}{2}$	. . .	" 360	

440 = *Amount of the debt.*   1,320 = *Sum of the products.*

Then 1,320 divided by 440 gives 3 years, which is the equated or average time of payment.

EXAMPLE 2.

Bought goods payable as follows, viz.: — $50 on the 1st of May; $64 on the 4th of June; $86 on the 1st of August; and $90 on the 5th of September. Required the equated time for paying the whole sum once?   *Ans.* July 14.

Dates.		*Amounts.*			
May 1st,	. . .	$50—*due at this date.**			
June 4th,	. . .	64 $\times$	34 days=	2,176	
Aug. 1st,	. . .	86 $\times$	92 " =	7,912	
Sept. 5th,	. . .	90 $\times$	127 " =	11,430	

$290   21,518 $\div$ 290 = 74 days.

21,518, the sum of the products, divided by 290, the amount of the debts, gives 74 days from the first of May, which is July 14th, the equated time.

---

* The equated time may be found by reckoning either from the present period, or from the time that the first payment becomes due. In the latter case, the time or multiplier of the *first* payment is nothing.

CASE II.

When goods are purchased at different periods, but at the same length of credit.

RULE. — Find the number of days * from the first to the second purchase. Multiply the amount of the second purchase by that number of days. Proceed in the same manner with respect to the third, and whatever other number of purchases there may be ; divide the sum of their products by the amount of purchases, and the quotient will be days. *Add* the days thus found to the date of the first purchase, and the time will be carried *forward* to the period of equation.

EXAMPLE.

Bought goods as follows at six months' credit. What is the average time of payment ?

Dates.		Sums.	Days.	Products.
May 1,	. . . . .	$ 50		
" 12,	. . . . .	150	$\times$ 11 =	1,650
" 19,	. . . . .	120	$\times$ 18 =	2,160
" 27,	. . . . .	100	$\times$ 26 =	2,600

$$6,410 \div 420 = 15\tfrac{11}{42} \text{ days,}$$

which, added to the 1st of May, carries *forward* the period of equation to the 16th of that month.

Proof. — Multiply the sum of each purchase made *before* the equated time, by the number of days from its date to the equated time. Multiply, also, separately, the amount of each purchase made *after* the equated time, by the number of days from the period of equation to the time it was made ; and if the sum of the former products be equal to the latter, the work is right, as is shown in the following operation : —

$$\$ 50 \times 15\tfrac{11}{42} = 763\tfrac{4}{42} \qquad \$120 \times 2\tfrac{31}{42} = 328\tfrac{24}{42}$$
$$150 \times 4\tfrac{11}{42} = 639\tfrac{12}{42} \qquad 100 \times 10\tfrac{31}{42} = 1,073\tfrac{34}{42}$$
$$\overline{\quad 1,402\tfrac{16}{42}\quad} \qquad\qquad \overline{\quad 1,402\tfrac{16}{42}\quad}$$

The foregoing illustration is so apparent, as to render any further explanation unnecessary.

CASE III.

When goods are purchased at different periods and at different terms of credit.

RULE. — Find the time when each amount becomes due, from which make an equation as in CASE II.

---

* The day *from* which you compute is not reckoned ; but the day *to* which you compute is *always included.*

EXAMPLE.

Bought goods as follows : — What is the equated time of payment for the whole amount ?   *Ans.* July 4

Dates.		Amounts.		Terms.
February 1,	. . . .	$100	. . . .	at 120 days.
" 15,	. . . .	150	. . . .	at 90 "
May 7,	. . . .	70	. . . .	at 60 "
August 12,	. . . .	90	. . . .	at 80 "

The purchase made

February 15, is due May 16,	. .	$150		
" 1, " June 1,	. . .	100 $\times$	16 $=$	1,600
May 7, " July 6,	. . .	70 $\times$	51 $=$	3,570
August 12, " Oct. 31,	. . .	90 $\times$	168 $=$	15,120
		$410		20,290

$20,290 \div 410 = 49\frac{20}{41}$ days from May 16, which will bring the equated time to July 4.

CASE IV.

When goods are bought at a given credit, and partial payments are made before the expiration of the stipulated term of credit, to know how long the balance may run to cancel the interest on the payments made before maturity.

RULE. — *First :* Multiply the whole debt by the term of credit given. *Second :* Multiply each payment before maturity, by the time it has run from the date of purchase, and subtract the amount of their products from the product arising from the whole debt multiplied by the term of credit. Divide the remainder by the balance due at the expiration of the term of credit, and the quotient will show the number of days that this balance may run from the time the sale was made.

EXAMPLE.

Bought goods, amounting to $2,500, at 12 months' credit. At the end of three months, there was paid $400; at the end of six months, $500; and at the end of eight months, $200. When will the balance of $1,400 become due?

$$2,500 \times 12 = 30,000$$

$400 \times 3 = 1,200$	
$500 \times 6 = 3,000$	
$200 \times 8 = 1,600$	
——	5,800
5,800	$24,200 \div 1,400 = 17\frac{2}{7}$ months.
$1,400 \times 17\frac{2}{7} = 24,200$	
Proof. 30,000	Q

CASE V.

To equate an account when there is a debit and credit of different amounts, and the total of each due at different periods, so that neither the debtor nor creditor shall be entitled to any balance of interest.

RULE. — *First:* Find the equated time of the *Dr.* and *Cr.* side, as before. *Second:* Multiply the *smallest* sum by the number of days between the dates, thus found, and divide the product by the *balance* of the account ; the quotient is the number of days to be carried back or forward, as the case may require.   ☞ If the *balance* be on the side of the EARLIEST date, *subtract* the quotient, or count *back* from that date ; if on the side of the LATEST date, *add* the quotient, or count *forward* from that date.

EXAMPLE 1.

A. B. owes me, for goods purchased at different periods, $600, which is due, by equation, May 1 ; and I have bought of him, at different dates, goods to the amount of $800, which is due, by equation, May 16. When shall I pay the balance so that neither party shall be entitled to interest ?   *Ans.* June 30.

$600 the smaller sum.
15 days, the difference of dates.
Balance, 200) 9,000 (45, the quotient.
9,000

The *balance*, in this example, is on the side of the *latest* date ; therefore *add* the quotient, or count *forward* 45 days from May 16, which brings the equated time to June 30.

Proof. — From May 16 to June 30 is 45 days × 800 = 3,600
From May 1 to June 30 is 60 days × 600 = 3,600

EXAMPLE 2.

C. D. owes me $600, which is due May 16, and I owe him 800, which is due May 1.   When must I pay the balance, $200, without either party being entitled to interest?   *Ans.* March 17.

$600 × 15 = 9,000 ÷ 200 = 45 days, which, subtracted from the 1st of May, will carry the time back to the 17th of March.

In this case, the amount of C. D.'s credit being greater than the amount of my debit, and being first payable, it is evident that interest will accrue from the 1st to the 16th of May on the amount of his credit, after which he will be entitled to the interest on $200 more than I shall, so long as the accounts from that time remain unsettled ; consequently, the longer the accounts run after the time of payment, the greater will be the balance of interest in C. D.'s favor ; but if the accounts be settled on the 17th of March, I shall pay C. D. $800, 45 days before it is due, and he will pay me $600, 60 days before it becomes payable, and the interest of both amounts for the time that they are paid in advance will be equal.

EXAMPLE 3.

Equate the time of payment of the debit and credit sides of the following account, and state when the balance becomes due, so that neither party shall be entitled to interest.

— *Dr.* — — A. B. — — *Cr.* —

When due.			*When due.*		
May 6,	To goods, .	$600	May 12,	By cash, .	$450
" 27,	" .	700	" 29,	" .	600
June 11,	" .	500	June 15,	" .	300
		$1,800			$1,350

$$600$$
$$700 \times 21 = 14,700$$
$$500 \times 36 = 18,000$$
$$\overline{32,700} \div 1,800 = 18 \text{ days from the 6th of May,}$$

will carry the time forward to the 24th of that month.

$$450$$
$$600 \times 17 = 10,200$$
$$300 \times 34 = 10,200$$
$$\overline{20,400} \div 1,350 = 15 \text{ days from the 12th of}$$

May, will carry the time forward to the 27th of that month.

— *Dr.* — — *Cr.* —
May 24, $1,800. *May* 27, $1,350.

$1,350 \times 3 = 4,050 \div 450 = 9$ days, which, subtracted from the 24th of May, will carry the time *back* to the 15th of the same month.

TABLE,

SHOWING THE NUMBER OF DAYS FROM ANY DAY IN ONE MONTH TO THE
SAME DAY IN ANOTHER MONTH.

To ☞ From	Jan.	Feb.	Mar.	April.	May.	June.	July.	Aug.	Sept.	Oct.	Nov.	Dec.
January....	365	31	59	90	120	151	181	212	243	273	304	334
February ...	334	365	28	59	89	120	150	181	212	242	273	303
March......	306	337	365	31	61	92	122	153	184	214	245	275
April	275	306	334	365	30	61	91	122	153	183	214	244
May.......	245	276	304	335	365	31	61	92	123	153	184	214
June.......	214	245	273	304	334	365	30	61	92	122	153	183
July.......	184	215	243	274	304	335	365	31	62	92	123	153
August.....	153	184	212	243	273	304	334	365	31	61	92	122
September ..	122	153	181	212	242	273	303	334	365	30	61	91
October	92	123	151	182	212	243	273	304	335	365	31	61
November ..	61	92	120	151	181	212	242	273	304	334	365	30
December ...	31	62	90	121	151	182	212	243	274	304	335	365

EXPLANATION. — The months counted *from* are arranged in the left-hand vertical column ; those counted *to* are in the upper horizontal line. The days between those periods are found in the angle of intersection, in the same way as in a common multiplication table. If the end of February be included between the two points of time, a day must be added in *leap years*.

Suppose it were required to know the number of days from the 4th of March to the 15th of August. In the *horizontal* line marked 'March,' and in the column under 'August,' we find 153, which is the number of days from the 4th (or any other) day of March to the 4th (or same) day of August ; but, as we want the time to the 15th of August, 11 days (the difference between 4 and 15) must be *added* to 153, which shows that 164 is the number of days between the 4th of March and the 15th of August.

Again, were the number of days required between the 10th of October and the 3d of June, in the following year : — Opposite to ' October,' and under ' June,' we find 243, which is the number of days from the 10th of October to the 10th of June ; but as we sought the time to the 3d only, which is 7 days earlier, we must *deduct* 7 from 243, leaving 236, the number of days required : — and so of others.

The above table will be found very useful in the equating the time of payments, calculating interest, &c., and, if not the best, is certainly the most concise, that has yet appeared on the subject.

Printed in the United Kingdom
by Lightning Source UK Ltd.
121638UK00001B/182/A